"*Mary Howard's book is a gift to teachers everywhere—a gift of alternatives to help us move from practices that don't work (and never have) to ones that transform us into the reflective, knowledgeable decision makers we must become.*"

—SHARON TABERSKI, AUTHOR OF *COMPREHENSION FROM THE GROUND UP*

"Good to Great Teaching *invites a heightened awareness of the range of practices that can help educators use instructional minutes with greater wisdom—finding more ways to teach smarter rather than work harder.*"

—LINDA HOYT, AUTHOR OF *CRAFTING NONFICTION PRIMARY*

"*Using authentic examples that illustrate how teachers are transforming their teaching through self-reflection, decision making, and action goals, Mary guides teachers through the process of critically examining their work and creating plans for improving their instructional practices.*"

—LINDA DORN, AUTHOR OF *INTERVENTIONS THAT WORK*

"*Mary focuses on helping teachers move from bad work, to good work, and then on to great work. Read this book, think hard about the ideas set forth, and then go work on becoming a teacher who does great work every day, all day.*"

—RICHARD L. ALLINGTON, PH.D., AUTHOR OF *WHAT REALLY MATTERS FOR STRUGGLING READERS*

Good to Great

to

TEACHING

Good *to* Great
TEACHING

Mary Howard

FOREWORD BY

Richard L. Allington

—————

FOCUSING
ON THE
LITERACY
WORK
THAT
MATTERS

HEINEMANN
Portsmouth, NH

Heinemann
361 Hanover Street
Portsmouth, NH 03801–3912
www.heinemann.com

Offices and agents throughout the world

The author and publisher wish to thank those who have generously given permission to reprint borrowed material:

Figure 4.6 is adapted from the "Model of Explicit Instruction" in "The Instruction of Reading Comprehension" by P. D. Pearson and M. C. Gallagher, originally appearing in *Contemporary Educational Psychology*, 1983, Volume 8, Issue 3. Published by Academic Press. Reprinted by permission of Copyright Clearance Center.

Library of Congress Cataloging-in-Publication Data
Howard, Mary.
   Good to great teaching : focusing on the literacy work that matters / Mary Howard ; foreword by Richard L. Allington.
     pp. cm.
   Includes bibliographical references.
   ISBN-13: 978-0-325-04369-2
   ISBN-10: 0-325-04369-8
   1. Language arts (Elementary).   2. Effective teaching.   I. Title.
   LB1576.H678 2012   2012012908
   372.6—dc23

Editor: Teva Blair
Production: Victoria Merecki
Typesetter: Gina Poirier Graphic Design
Cover and interior designs: Lisa A. Fowler
Front cover photo: Lesley Scheele
Manufacturing: Steve Bernier

Printed in the United States of America on acid-free paper
16 15   VP   3 4 5

This book is dedicated to

*Marie Clay for showing me
the meaning of great work,
Linda Hoyt for encouraging me
to write about great work,
and the students and teachers
who inspire great work!*

Table of Contents

To download the forms featured throughout this book and a free study guide, please visit www.heinemann.com/products/E04369.aspx and click on the Companion Resources tab.

*W*hen I read Mary Howard's first book, *RTI from All Sides,* I knew I had found another book on Response to Intervention (RTI) that I could recommend educators read. That book, unlike so many books on RTI, was filled with exceptionally good teaching advice and exceptionally practical assessment advice. In this new book I found content that was just as exceptional—though here she focuses on helping teachers move from bad work to good work, and then on to great work. She does this through the stories of individual teachers who are each working to become teachers who do great work every day, every lesson.

Mary Howard is a bit like the "guide on the side" as you read this book. She has developed a number of reflective forms to support you in moving from bad to good to great work every day. I can see the book being studied as an individual attempts to promote the development of exemplary instruction. I can see the book as a faculty read in some schools where everyone is working to provide great teaching all day every day. I can see literacy coaches using the book to help guide their efforts at supporting the development of more effective teachers. I can see principals reading it to foster the development of their expertise about what great teaching looks like.

I've written a lot about the exemplary first- and fourth-grade teachers we studied (Allington 2002; Allington and Johnston 2002; Allington, Johnston, and Day 2002). I mention this because what Mary Howard captures in this short text is the equivalent of how to become an exemplary teacher. One of the things we learned in our study was that exemplary teachers are not born but rather they are created, created by systems of support that move them from bad practice to good practice and then to great practice. The exemplary teachers we studied told us they could never have become great teachers had it not been for a mentor, typically another teacher who helped them along the way to greatness. They also told us about their first years of teaching, before they had developed into great teachers and how good it felt to realize that every year brought them closer to great practice all the time.

So read this book, think hard about the ideas set forth, and then go work on becoming a teacher who does great work every day, all day.

Richard L. Allington, Ph.D.
Professor of Literacy Studies

*T*here's an old saying that life is what happens when we aren't looking. That seems an apt description of my entry into the writing arena. I am eternally grateful to Linda Hoyt and Wendy Murray for a gentle nudge into a new world I have come to treasure. My world revolves around real teachers and real children. I am *not* a researcher or university professor. I *am* a teacher deeply devoted to literacy excellence, talented teachers making responsible choices where it matters most, and countless students who deserve nothing less than great work every minute of every day.

Thank you to Michael Bungay Stanier for a tiny book that inadvertently gave life to an idea simmering in my mind for years. His work sparked my passionate quest for *great work*. I am grateful to brilliant researchers and educators who so generously shared their thoughts about great work in the pages of this book: Richard Allington, Linda Dorn, Ellin Keene, Gretchen Owocki, Linda Hoyt, Tim Rasinski, Sharon Taberski, Gail Moser, Joan Boushey, Kouider Mokhtari, Kelly Boswell, Jane Olson, Jamie Berry, Kelly Davis, and Rick Wormeli. The insight expressed in their words of wisdom has once again supported my lifelong exploration of great work in abundance.

Each step of this book has been an exciting journey, but I will forever recall the very second I received a foreword from the remarkable Dr. Richard Allington. I have been one of the many lucky recipients of his vast knowledge for the past forty years so seeing his name grace my book is a personal dream come true. Thank you for helping me understand what great work in literacy is all about, Dr. Allington. You are my hero!

The support of the Heinemann family has truly been a blessing. My editor and friend, Teva Blair, championed this book from the beginning stages and gently guided me in turning my vision into a reality. Her expert tutelage nurtured a writer still struggling to break free and fueled excitement even when uncertainty and insecurity threatened to cloud my thinking. I'm so proud to be part of such a talented group and grateful for their support each step of the way from writing, editing, revising, formatting, book production, and marketing. Sarah Fournier, Victoria Merecki, and Valerie McNally made the final stages an exciting process with their unwavering support and wisdom. Lisa Fowler once again worked her magic to turn a cover into a work of art that proves a picture really is worth a thousand words. Thank you also to Gina Poirier for the typesetting that brought

Lisa Fowler's beautful text design to life. I'm in awe of the talented graciousness that simply abounds at Heinemann and I am so grateful to be the benefactor of their gifts.

I'm not sure how to even begin to properly thank the dedicated educators who graciously opened their doors to shared collaborations that turned into friendships. I couldn't have selected better schools with which to share my passionate journey to great work. "Thank you" seems inadequate for breathing life into each page of this book. My deepest admiration to the talented staff at:

Sunapee Central Elementary School; Sunapee, New Hampshire
Administrator: Alan Pullman; reading/writing specialist: Jo Skarin
Special thanks to librarian, Tracey Koehler, for photography support.

Mustang Elementary School; Mustang, Oklahoma
Administrator: Laquita Semmler; reading specialist: Jackie Stafford

Sunset Terrace Elementary; Rochester, Minnesota
Administrators: Jody Goldstein (principal), Shari Engel (administrative assistant);
reading specialists: Jamie Berry and Dawn Schuster

A special thank-you to Nita Wood's third-grade students in Mustang, Oklahoma, for sharing their love of writing with me. Their thoughtful questions helped me think about writing in new ways. You made me a better and more confident writer by helping me look at writing through *your* eyes. Keep writing, boys and girls!

I am fortunate to have the support of an amazing family. To my best friend and sister, Sandy; amazing brothers and ardent supporters, Jim, John, and Mike; nieces by birth but children by heart, Tracey, Kristin, and Cyndi; and nieces and nephews Austin, Brittyn, Barrett, Carlee, Codie, Cole, Dan, Daniel, Elliot, Jude, Julian, Kendall, Kenzie, Madeline, Moses, Rachel, Rick, and Simon.

I wrote much of the first draft of this book in Honolulu, Hawaii where I met an amazing young man. Tai was so excited to learn I was writing a book. Later that morning, he approached me in a restaurant to ask for my autograph. He lovingly held a book as he talked about books he loves. I was inspired by this young book lover and realized he was the real reason for writing this book. I wondered if his love of reading was acknowledged and supported with the thoughtful instructional opportunities he so richly deserved.

I think about my brief encounter with Tai often and hope the ideas in this book are a priority in his school. Tai deserves the same successful, enthusiastic opportunities and I hope his life is filled with teachers who make great work the standard we should all work to achieve. We owe it to Tai and to every child we are lucky enough to have in our care, regardless of what they may bring to the literacy table. They deserve great work *every* day in *every* classroom *every* year.

Thank you for reminding me, Tai! Aloha and Mahalo!

Take My Advice

From World War II
That made world history—
To the planets unknown mysteries
From the knights who fought for the fair maiden—
To the deserts biggest canyons . . .

Pages will reveal all the questions
That need to be answered
You will always get lost in a book
No matter what chapter or page
It doesn't matter if you are on page 32 or chapter 2
You will feel lost in every which way
Just take my advice:
Reading is the answer to everything
If you are determined
You will blossom and grow

Written by Maddy Hynes
Mrs. Scheele's Grade 5 class

66 *Never doubt that a small group of thoughtful committed citizens can change the world. Indeed, it's the only thing that ever has."*

—Margaret Mead

I close my eyes and envision classrooms ablaze with active literacy where passionate and intellectual endeavors are woven into a single patchwork. I see children read books they can and choose to read with enthusiastic conversations and purposeful instruction in great abundance. I see children experience success all day long through coordinated learning opportunities. I see assessment and instruction inseparably entwined in an interrelated process. I see teachers willingly make challenging choices in the name of students. And looming above it all, I see teachers committed to *responsive thoughtful instruction*—the heartbeat of the literacy work that matters.

Maddy's joyous description of reading as a way to "blossom and grow" in her opening poem epitomizes this view. But Maddy's entry into this world did not happen by chance or due to meaningless activities. Maddy perceives reading as the *answer to everything* because enthusiastic authentic literacy is her reality. It can also be our reality *if* we are willing to heed Maddy's heartfelt advice.

But is Maddy's advice feasible in a world where decision making has become an instructional tug-of-war? Can we win a battle of wits as control is slowly whittled away from those who make the decisions that matter most? The answer is a resounding "yes" *if* we are insistent participants in bringing this world to life. Knowledgeable teachers with a fervent commitment to the literacy work that matters have always been our best hope.

This is undoubtedly the best of times and the worst of times. We have amassed an instructional arsenal of literacy research support that will allow professional knowledge and classroom practice to work in concert. Some of us have been seduced by recipes, while others know quick fixes are rarely in the best interest of students but feel powerless to fight that battle. With money limited and advice plentiful, we may struggle to find the time, resources, or support to do the job we want desperately to do. Too often, we feel inadequate in spite of a vast body of knowledge or we aren't afforded the professional learning opportunities that would surely elevate our teaching to the highest levels.

There's good news. The world I describe is within any teacher's reach. This book is written for teachers who believe they still make the choices that matter and refuse to let anything stand in their way to do so. It is for teachers who address limited time in the day by reallocating that time in far better ways. It is for teachers ready to take back the reigns of instructional decision making. It is for teachers willing to put children ahead of politics or agendas. It is for each of you reading these words at this very moment.

So how do we accomplish this? How do we ensure our students' days are filled with successful literacy opportunities? How do we put our students' needs above grade-level mandates? We do this by *choosing* to allow only relevant, meaningful experiences into our day. We do this by *choosing* learning experiences that have the greatest outcome. And we do this by *choosing* to make personal professional learning a priority—even if we have to initiate these opportunities on our own. These are the responsible *choices* excellent teachers make every day—*choices* that reflect the very essence of this book.

I was recently rushing to a flight when a picture in an art display from a local school caught my eye. It was the most beautiful drawing of large open hands holding many small children. I was astonished to find that a fifth grader had created it. As I moved closer, I noticed faint pencil marks and erasures beneath the perfect drawing. I thought about the trial-and-error perseverance that must have gone into this diligent pursuit. Suddenly, I felt a rush of pride for the anonymous art teacher who must have supported that extraordinary move toward imperfect perfection each step of the way.

Jazz musician great Ornette Coleman said, "It was when I found out that I could make mistakes that I was on to something." This is directly applicable to our teaching, as some of the most important instructional successes have been borne out of failure. In the end, it is our successes rather than our mistakes that matter. But those successes require us to go through a period of discomfort that is inevitable as we turn tentative pencil marks and deliberate erasures into a colorful landscape of instructional possibilities.

Seth Godin calls this period of discomfort the dip, or an inevitable sinkhole that can trip us up (2007). When we are in a dip, we can quit or we can put forth the extra effort that will ultimately lead us to success. A cul-de-sac is simply a dead end that saps valuable time and energy, while the dip leads to success if we can weather the storm and whittle away at it bit by bit. Godin refers to this as strategic quitting and he advises: "Quit the wrong stuff. Stick with the right stuff. Have the guts to do one or the other" (4).

Godin makes a profound point with his description of hardworking woodpeckers: "A woodpecker can tap twenty times on a thousand trees and get nowhere, but stay busy. Or he can tap twenty thousand times on one tree and get dinner" (29). If we continue to put our effort into doing a multitude of different things that are not working, we will have little time and energy left to focus on the literacy work that matters.

This is particularly important given the diverse needs in today's classrooms. Some teachers feel like "tightrope walkers without a safety net" (Buffum et al. 2010). But there's no shortcut across that tightrope. As noted by Tomlinson, "Excellent teachers never fall prey to the belief that they are good enough. The best teachers I have known are humbled by how much more they need to learn" (2010/2011, 24). These teachers actively seek learning opportunities in great volume whether this critical goal is honored in their school or not. This book is a personal professional development opportunity if you are willing to do the hard work required to achieve excellence.

How to Use the Forms in This Book

Throughout this book you will find a number of problem-solving forms designed to slow down your teaching through thoughtful reflection. All of these forms are available for download at www.heinemann.com/products/E04369.aspx (click on the Companion Resources tab). These tools will help to critique your instructional choices and how those

choices affect students in positive or negative ways. Within a heightened sense of awareness for the quality of our work, we will omit, add, or adjust our practices based on the
benefit they afford our students. This is not about doing more or harder work. It's about
making smarter choices so our time is spent in the most effective ways.

To ensure the forms are used in the spirit intended, keep these things in mind:

- Use each suggested form as you read the instructional descriptions. This will allow
  you to experience this process through others before you apply it on your own.
- While we will explore practices to alleviate, always view your teaching through a
  positive lens. Identify what you're already doing well and do more of it.
- These are personal reflection tools, not evaluative forms. They are designed for
  introspection and dialogue, not for pointing fingers.
- Put the forms in a notebook to revisit over the course of the year. There is great
  power in looking at our successes along the way or repeating a form.
- Select those forms that are relevant to your goals at that time. Use them in any
  order to set instructional priorities and eliminate any that are no longer needed.
- Be specific in identifying goals. Set a numerical goal to reduce worksheets or
  describe what you will do with time saved sitting at your desk. Be crystal clear.
- Highlight what you do using students as a measurement marker. Their success or
  failure is our responsibility, so always consider your role in this process.
- Engaging dialogue in a supportive environment elevates forms. Consider doing
  them with trusted colleagues in positive professional interactions.
- It's helpful to limit your reflection to one teaching focus. Narrow the scope by
  exploring one aspect of the literacy block or learning activity.

We're about to launch into a shared journey of reflective decision making. In
Chapter 1, I'll define terms to build a solid framework for the literacy work that matters.
In Chapter 2, we'll initiate goals that offer a sense of direction and instructional focus. In
Chapter 3, we'll take a closer look at our struggling readers to create a literacy program
that will accommodate specific student needs. In Chapter 4, we'll look at a flexible, inclusive learning design that embraces all students. In Chapter 5, we'll consider the dual
nature of instruction and assessment that impacts both students and teachers. Finally,
in Chapter 6 we'll reflect on the changes you've made as you have worked through these
pages and explore how you can continue to enhance and sustain your great work.

Preparing to Focus on the Literacy Work that Matters

Director Baz Luhrman's 1996 song from Romeo and Juliet, *Everybody's Free (to Wear Sunscreen)*, is happiness advice. Perhaps I should have added the best advice to my cover: "Warning: You will be asked to do one thing that scares you every day!"

In 2009, I did the scariest thing I've ever done when I wrote my first book, *RTI from All Sides: What Every Teacher Needs to Know* (Howard 2009). My plunge headfirst into unfamiliar and terrifying territory was a leap of faith that led to a second book, *Moving Forward with RTI: Reading and Writing Activities for Every Instructional Setting and Tier* (Howard 2010), and now the book you are holding in your hands. Luckily, each one has been accomplished with an increasingly healthy level of angst.

You see, doing something that scares us every day allows us to slowly chip away our fears as the initial discomfort dissipates. From an instructional perspective, we have two choices. We can accept the status quo or we can change our little corner of the world. Sitting back in passive compliance is simply unacceptable because the repercussions are too frightening to consider. I hope you opt to join me as we work together to change our little corner of the world. One teacher can set an amazing domino effect in motion.

I am *not* a researcher and this is *not* a research manual. I am a teacher and this book reflects my insatiable curiosity about literacy and my dedication to children, saturated in a vast research map to guide my way. I didn't just write this book—I lived this book. It's based on my work with real teachers and children. I was a willing participant in a passionate investigation doing precisely what I ask of you. I faced the same challenges, tackled the same frustrations, and celebrated the same achievements. Teachers and children breathed life into this book over the course of one year as we worked side by side, and it is my gift to respected comrades.

So grab a cup of coffee. Slip off your shoes. Get comfortable. Imagine we're huddled in a corner of your classroom engaged in lively dialogue revolving around a shared vision for high-quality literacy. I am beside you supporting your efforts to engage students in literacy experiences that will help every child soar to great heights. This is one battle we cannot afford to lose. I think it's a worthy battle. A worthy battle indeed, my friend!

CHAPTER 1

Building a Common Understanding for Bad Work, Good Work, and Great Work

66 *Great Work is what we all want more of. This is the work that is meaningful to you, that has an impact and makes a difference. It inspires, stretches, and provokes. Great Work is the work that matters."*

(Stanier 2010, 5)

Let's begin with a little experiment. Go ahead—trust me. Close your eyes and take a deep breath. Closed? Relaxed? Ready? Now reach back into the inner recesses of your memory and recall a time you were truly engaged in a thoroughly fulfilling learning experience. It doesn't matter what or when as long as it conjures an abundance of fond memories. Elementary? High School? College? The School of Life? Got it? Good. Stop and savor those images, impressions, and events. Hold it . . .

Nice work! Now list any descriptive words that reflect those positive images, impressions, and events dancing in your memory stream. Jot down whatever comes to mind. Don't worry. There are no right or wrong answers. Just free your mind and bask in the joy of the experience. When you finish, review your list. Go ahead, I'll wait.

Now let me tell you what is *not* on your list. I'm willing to bet *no* worksheets without value or purpose warmed the cockles of your heart; *no* round-robin of stumbled reading for an impatient audience made you leap with unbridled joy; *no* images of books void of meaning called forth visions of rainbows on the horizon. I'm 100 percent certain descriptors like boring, frustrating, and embarrassing are *not* on your list.

Then one haunting question should form a dark cloud hovering above us. If these things aren't remotely related to what we know about thoroughly fulfilling learning experiences, why would we let even one intrude upon our day? What alternatives reflect the enthusiastic, meaningful, and purposeful learning our students need and deserve? How can we gain access to those things and more in an already full day? These questions are the heart and soul of this book.

As I look back on my teaching over the past four decades, two life-changing events stand out. The first was my Reading Recovery training that continues to drive my thinking about literacy. The second was the day I inadvertently stumbled on a little book that had an immediate and profound impact on my work with teachers and children.

Do More Great Work (Stanier 2010) is a business book that has forever altered my thinking as a literacy teacher. Stanier lives in a business world where financial stakes are high, but our stakes are even higher—the literate lives of children. The message that resonates in Stanier's book is that we must do more great work in any endeavor and his subtitle reads like a heartfelt plea: *Stop the Busywork, and Start the Work that Matters.*

Stanier borrows from graphic designer Milton Glaser (2008), explaining that our work falls into three categories: bad work, good work, or great work. Categories help us evaluate the quality of our work, although this is more complex than labeling since the designation of a category may change according to the situation and the participants involved. But the act of categorizing our work initiates a reflection process that can help us grow as we consider our choices more deeply so they can become more intentional.

Using this concept as our vessel, we are about to embark on an exciting journey together. I packed an unwavering devotion to literacy, an intricate web of experiences, a wealth of research translated into practice, an acute awareness that professional learning is never-ending, and a deep respect for the work you do in the trenches. All you need is the dedication to do whatever it takes to help *every* student achieve literacy success. This book is a celebration of *you* no matter how long you have taught, how busy you are, how overwhelmed you feel, or how much support surrounds you. Welcome aboard!

I should warn you this trip is not for the fainthearted. I will ask you to reflect upon and evaluate your practices. I will ask you to question those practices even if it evokes discomfort. I will ask you to eliminate anything that wastes time to make room for those things that are a better use of time and then raise the bar to take your teaching even higher. In return, I'll respect your role as captain of our ship and keep you in safe waters at all times. If you're up for this challenge, roll up your sleeves and assume your rightful position at the helm. It's full steam ahead.

General Overview of Bad Work, Good Work, and Great Work

So let's begin with a quick look at bad work, good work, and great work.

Bad Work

Bad work is anything that saps the time and energy needed for good work and great work. Bad work has little or no payoff so it's a frivolous time-wasting event that usurps precious minutes that many students can ill afford. Bad work is usually easy and requires limited effort or thought from teachers or students. It's empty calories with no nutritional value. It's the Pac-Man of excellence, voraciously eating its way across our day and sapping the resources for the work that matters. Bad work is, well, bad.

Good Work

Good work is good by definition. We need good work since it benefits students (how we determine the value of our work). In fact, good work often leads to great work if we can make adjustments that elevate our work. I suspect most great work is borne from good work since great work takes time and effort. We want more good work because the payoff to students is high. The only problem with good work is that it takes the time and energy we need for great work. Good work is good—but it's not great.

Great Work

Great work is the most challenging to define, but I suspect you don't need an explanation if you've ever experienced it. Great work takes our teaching to the highest level and offers the most benefit to our students. Great work happens when teachers cautiously translate research principles into practice so it requires more effort in the early stages. Those who do great work develop an insatiable appetite and want to savor the experience over and over. Great work lights up a room with energy and enthusiasm.

Now that we have a general overview of these categories, let's fine-tune our understanding from an instructional perspective. Categorizing our work isn't an either/or proposition since many factors can alter our selection. Reflection gives us a forum to verbalize our thinking so we can make intentional choices how to best spend our limited available time. As we examine our practices, we can navigate toward more great work through a flexible decision-making process based on the benefit to students.

Examining Our Practices More Closely for Evidence of Bad Work

The term "bad work" is not meant in a negative light or to label events and teachers as "bad." Rather, exploring our teaching for evidence of bad work helps us reflect more critically on the many choices in our control and how these choices affect students. Some bad work gobbles precious minutes while some is simply less effective, less productive, or less valuable than an alternative. Good teachers consistently question the value of their work and change the trajectory of that work if it conflicts with high-quality literacy. Noticing bad work doesn't make us bad teachers. To the contrary, the ability to notice and modify bad work makes us highly qualified, knowledgeable, and responsible teachers who maintain control of our own decision making in the name of student learning.

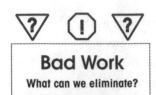

FIGURE 1.1 **Great work begins by alleviating anything that usurps valuable time**

Every teacher does bad work and anyone who says they don't is delusional. Even the best teachers I've ever had the pleasure to witness in glorious action would admit to bad work (I have a personal history of bad work, although it rears its ugly head less often these days). The distinction is that they do bad work less frequently, recognize it more quickly, and are more likely to resolve it. As we become more adept in recognizing bad work, we become increasingly insistent about altering questionable practices where it matters most. If we refuse to do so, it's intentional bad work—the worst kind.

Bad work is a chameleon that changes according to interpretation or intent, so we must be brutally honest as we evaluate our work. Reflective introspection allows us to initiate external or internal dialogue to deepen our understanding. We begin to recognize that one can do bad work extremely well, making it good bad work. We don't explore bad work to label people or events, but to notice it when it happens so we can use that time in more productive ways in the future. It's just that simple!

The chart on page 5 includes some descriptors and examples of this category.

We must be able to recognize evidence of bad work and then eliminate it in order to do good work or great work. Bad work can occur in the blink of an eye, or over an extended period. Bad work may be intentional due to a personal choice or unintentional due to inadequate knowledge or experience. Some things consistently reflect bad work, while others fluctuate depending on circumstances. Sadly, bad work we fail to acknowledge and resolve over time can cause great emotional and intellectual harm.

Bad work can often be elevated with simple adjustments or substitutions. Brief, meaningful drawings help students reflect on learning. Well-selected paper-pencil

AN OVERVIEW OF BAD WORK	
Descriptors of Bad Work	**Examples of Bad Work**
Anything that wastes valuable time due to: • frustrating texts and tasks • failure to offer adequate modeling • lack of support in the early stages • empty play over authentic literacy • ignoring crucial literacy research • skill and drill without application • mere assigning over teaching • rigid adherence to scripts or guides • getting sidetracked without purpose • ignoring student need	• passive worksheets • round-robin reading • irrelevant computer tasks • fill-in-the-blank, circle, underline • teacher sitting passively at desk • one-size-fits-all grade-level texts • trivial games and activities • crosswords or search-and-find puzzles • cut-and-paste or meaningless coloring • "stuff" over substance (learning) We could include anything that robs time from active literacy engagement

tasks offer a tool for classroom discussions. Purposeful oral reading is useful to prove, refute, or highlight a point. Passive worksheets may be substituted with student-created sticky notes in a visual display. A teacher sitting passively at a desk can rotate in order to listen to or confer with students. It's not hard to elevate bad work if we recognize it and are willing to alter or replace it with more effective options.

Examining Our Practices More Closely for Evidence of Good Work and Great Work

Good work and great work are alternatives that are a better use of time. We label bad work solely to use the time we save in more effective ways. Bad work can creep up on us when we least expect it, so we must become hypervigilant so that we can notice if it happens. Bad work can occur if we are not knowledgeable about quality literacy and fail to connect research and practice, while good

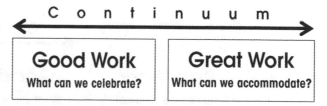

FIGURE 1.2 **Our teaching can move along a continuum between good work and great work**

work and great work require us to adhere to these things. Bad work stands alone while good work and great work are on a continuum where the lines of distinction may blur.

Good work and great work are both desirable, but great work is more desirable. We increase or decrease the quality of our work as we move across this continuum. Good work has payoff but great work has more payoff. Good work benefits students but great work benefits them more. Excuse my intentional grammatical faux pas, but good work is good while great work is "gooder," as reflected in the chart below.

AN OVERVIEW OF GOOD WORK/GREAT WORK	
Descriptors of Good/Great Work	**Examples of Good/Great Work**
Anything that reinforces or extends learning: • active literacy engagement • access to high success texts • gradual release of teacher support • flexible grouping options • less emphasis on whole-class work • peer collaboration opportunities • ongoing independent application • teacher-supported problem solving • emphasis on strategic knowledge • integration across content areas	• rich literacy environment • classroom reading library • daily engagement in literacy • read-aloud/write-aloud • shared reading/writing • guided reading/writing • independent reading/writing • focus on reading, writing, and talking We can include anything that actively engages students in meaningful literacy

Good work and great work reside on a slippery slope—we can shift back and forth in a split second. Great work can be quickly reduced to good work and good work can be quickly elevated to great work. This occurs if we fail to notice or take advantage of a teachable moment. Good work and great work often require thoughtful planning, but it can also

FIGURE 1.3 **The interplay between bad, good, and great work**

occur in the heat of the moment—moving around the room if attention fades, generating questions to engage students, drawing attention to a key idea, conducting a strategy think-aloud, or letting students turn and talk to verbalize their thinking. These split-second decisions can quickly move us between good work and great work.

There is a rich interplay between these categories. The more we know what constitutes bad work, the more we understand good work. The more we know what constitutes good work, the more we can move to great work. As bad work occurs less frequently, we gain understandings that transform good work to great work. Once we understand great work, we hunger for more. This is a learning curve at its best.

To understand what this looks like, let's peek into a classroom to see how our choices diminish or elevate teaching and learning. As you read, think about the wide range of intentional choices Mrs. Jones makes throughout this learning activity and how these choices impact the quality of her work.

Instructional Scenario 1: Initial Teaching Sequence

Mrs. Jones stands at the front of her third-grade class as students sit at their desks with a copy of the book. The story is part of a grade-level anthology with fascinating details of ocean animals to support their ongoing investigation of the topic. She begins by writing three questions on the board, telling students to look for clues to answer these questions as they read. Students then take turns reading orally as peers follow along. Mrs. Jones stops periodically to ask questions from a teacher's guide and others that rise from her interactions with students or her instincts as an experienced teacher. Some students read orally with expressive ease while others struggle painfully. The wide variations of student engagement are also glaringly obvious. Raul appears frustrated while Tamara peruses several pages ahead. Suzanne is lost in the photographs as Robert plays nervously with his pencil. Mrs. Jones doesn't appear to notice these behaviors from the front of the room. At one point, she draws attention to a compound word in the story and they stop to look for other examples to list on the board before they read on. When they finish, she asks them to discuss their learning with a partner and respond in a writing journal. When Todd asks if he can add a picture, she reminds them that writers express ideas in many ways and encourages them to do the same. As they work, she moves to her desk.

Now note your thinking in the columns (see Figure 1.4). This is not about labeling Mrs. Jones a bad teacher since she did many wonderful things. It's about developing a heightened sense of awareness for choices that impact students in positive or negative ways. Notice bad work that is less effective and good work or great work that enhances learning.

Evidence of Bad Work	Evidence of Good Work	Evidence of Great Work

FIGURE 1.4 **Categorizing Mrs. Jones' Initial Teaching Sequence**

I asked teachers I work with to consider how Mrs. Jones' choices hinder or support learning. Our success is always measured by our students' success, so we are unsuccessful if even *one* student is unsuccessful. As you look at these examples, keep in mind this process is designed to initiate a dialogue about the quality of our work rather than simply to label it. Consider how these examples may vary from your own thinking.

Bad Work

- "one-size-fits-all" grade-level text in spite of varied reading ranges
- round-robin reading (passive behaviors, students struggle publicly)
- focus on compound words to the point it may have sidetracked learning
- passively sitting at the desk as students work unsupported

Good Work

- high-interest topic integrated across the curriculum (science)
- limited number of key questions based on important ideas (three)
- designated questions in the teacher's guide used selectively
- time to collaborate with peers for the purpose of sharing learning

Great Work

- connecting to prior learning goals (ocean animals)
- establishing a clear purpose in writing that is consistently revisited
- flexibly generating questions based on interaction with students
- integration of writing using a journal activity with purposeful drawings

Considering the goal is student success, let's reflect on a few ways Mrs. Jones could have better supported Raul, Tamara, Suzanne, and Robert.

- use varied reading material rather than a one-size-fits-all text
- create an anchor chart or learning display to support ongoing learning
- initiate flexible small-group reading activities with texts matched to students
- avoid round-robin reading and opt for students to read silently or softly
- avoid getting sidetracked from the task at hand with unrelated tasks
- rotate as students work on their own to offer support or assess

Now we'll apply these ideas in a new instructional scenario. As you read, notice modifications that increased success for Raul, Tamara, Suzanne, and Robert and record what you notice in the chart (see Figure 1.5).

Instructional Scenario 2: Follow-Up Teaching Sequence

Mrs. Jones uses a variety of alternate texts for this literacy activity. She previously shared a whole-class read-aloud to introduce the topic of ocean animals and students have initiated a class chart. Today, she begins with a shared reading of an engaging poem on sharks. After reading, she asks students to look for facts they can add to the class wall display on ocean animals and records the vocabulary words they will revisit later. She displays a large piece of paper and draws attention to several containers of books about ocean animals at varied reading levels. Mrs. Jones explains that students will select a book of their choice to use in a small-group investigation. As she distributes sticky notes, she asks students to record new facts that will be added to the chart. Students begin working as she calls four students to the small-group table in the back corner of the room. They open a newsmagazine to an article on sharks, taking a few minutes to explore the colorful photographs. She reminds them to look for interesting facts to add to their sticky notes later. Students read brief portions silently as she listens to an individual child read aloud. After each section, they discuss learning and add key ideas to sticky notes. At one point, she draws attention to a compound word and quickly writes it on the board to add to their compound word chart later. When students finish, they return to work in their groups and she then calls five more students to take a spot at the back table with a new book on the same topic. After reading, they return to their seats to work in groups as Mrs. Jones rotates. She periodically pauses to discuss learning with students, briefly recording observations she will add to individual student folders later.

Evidence of Bad Work	Evidence of Good Work	Evidence of Great Work

FIGURE 1.5 **Categorizing Mrs. Jones' Follow-Up Teaching Sequence**

What increased the quality of this lesson? How successful do you think Raul, Tamara, Suzanne, and Robert will be in this scenario? What did Mrs. Jones do differently that had a direct impact on the quality of her lesson? What choices did she make that elevated both teaching and learning? In the end, *we* make the choices that matter!

Spotlight Teachers: The Literacy Work that Matters in Action

Now that we have a common understanding for bad work, good work, and great work in a fictional setting, let's see what this looks like in real settings. Throughout this book, I'll transport you into classrooms of new and veteran educators in Oklahoma, New Hampshire, and Minnesota where "spotlight" teachers will model a reflective process of change. You are cordially invited to join our conversations using two approaches.

1. In some cases, I observe a lesson first and use the teaching as a springboard to change. The teacher then applies new learning based on our discussion in a follow-up related lesson. These two sequences reflect the lesson variations.

2. In other cases, we discuss a teacher's lesson goals and make adjustments to the instructional plan prior to the lesson. The teacher then applies the changes based on our discussion in a single-lesson activity.

The wonderful spotlight teachers in this book are not meant to reflect perfection. Great work is in a constant state of flux according to the teacher, goals, situation, and learners. *What* these remarkable teachers do is much less important than *how* they make intentional choices to increase the quality of their own work. Good to great teaching is a personal growth process that varies from teacher to teacher. This is not about perfection, but how we consistently make relevant choices that will move us to improved practices.

So let's begin in three classrooms at Sunapee Central Elementary in Sunapee, New Hampshire. In this chapter, our spotlight teachers use two instructional sequences to categorize and enhance their teaching. You'll see our first reflection form in action as you practice on your own (see Figure 1.13). The forms in this book are carefully designed tools to reflect on, categorize, and adjust your teaching. It will be very helpful to complete the forms using the spotlight teacher descriptions before you apply them in your own teaching.

Let's begin with fifth-grade teacher Lesley Scheele. Lesley has taught for thirteen years. She is dedicated to independent and teacher-supported literacy. Her small-group lesson takes place in the first week of school because she has made this her priority.

SPOTLIGHT
TEACHER

Lesley Scheele, Grade 5:
Initial Teaching Sequence

Lesley calls five students to the small-group table. A quick look around the room reflects all students actively engaged in independent literacy. Lesley distributes a news-magazine article about spirit bears to students, knowing informational texts will entice them. She introduces it with enthusiasm, stating excitedly, "I can't wait to read about this topic." Lesley states her purpose of self-questioning, saying, "As we read, think about any questions that come to mind." The open-ended form she gives students supports her purpose and gives them a concrete tool. She tells students they can read and then write or write as they read, acknowledging her respect for their way of learning. As students suggest questions, she reinforces their ideas and encourages them to answer their own question or that of a peer. She repeatedly confirms the purpose with her own ponderings—"I'm wondering about . . . "—and encourages students to do the same. She compliments their ideas as they use schema or make connections to other learning. As students read silently and respond on the form, Lesley discusses the selection with individual students. Each student has an opportunity to share their ideas as others work on their own. There is never a lull as everyone, including

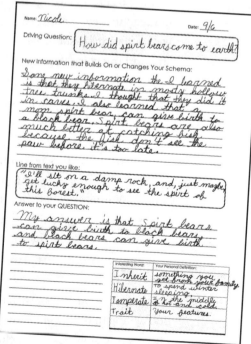

FIGURE 1.6 **Too many focus points can reduce the benefit of a form**

FIGURE 1.7 **Lesley promotes independent problem-solving and uses this time to support or observe students as they actively engage in learning**

Lesley, is intensely engaged at all times. She moves seamlessly between reading, writing, and talking, noticing when her students use effective strategies and responding to their efforts. She consistently shares her observations and encourages students to verbalize their thinking. Lesley transforms into a reader alongside her students, offering varied degrees of support, modeling her thinking, and encouraging them to engage in independent problem-solving as she waits in the wings. She uses the text as a resource to prove or support thinking with supportive language like, "That's fascinating," "I like your thinking," and "Good job using your schema." She repeatedly draws their attention to the purpose for reading, using the text.

Debriefing Session

Lesley did so many outstanding things I could highlight in our discussion. Her awareness increases the potential to do these things intentionally in the future, so I began our discussion by emphasizing effective practices already in place with simple tweaks to elevate her teaching even more. I don't *tell* teachers what to do, but *suggest* what may be invisible without another set of eyes and ears. In a sense, this reflective feedback process is like a "behind the glass" lesson without the glass (Clay 1985).

We discussed four simple ideas Lesley could apply in the next teaching sequence:

- The open-ended paper-and-pencil task may have too many points to think about. The form should reflect her stated purpose of self-questioning.

- Self-questioning is important for every student. A class anchor chart can be used to introduce this focus initially during a whole-class minilesson.

- Students generated wonderful questions but they had difficulty recalling them later. Writing questions on sticky notes will provide a helpful memory tool.

- Lesley wanted time to meet with other students. Selecting key stopping points as students are writing is a good time to quickly visit with others.

Lesley completed the top section of our first reflection form as we discussed her lesson (see Figure 1.13). She plans to apply these suggestions in the next sequence with a new group of students. I wish every teacher had the opportunity afforded Lesley, but anyone willing to reflect honestly on one's own teaching can achieve this move to great work. The key is to slow down and closely examine your teaching to make improvements. Lesley uses our form to ponder her transformation between lesson sequences.

FIGURE 1.8 **Lesley introduces a class anchor chart that will support learning in varied settings**

Follow-Up Teaching Sequence

Lesley begins in a whole-group setting to initiate an instructional springboard for small-group and independent seatwork. She conducts a ten-minute minilesson on self-questioning using a carefully selected read-aloud to create an anchor chart as a concrete tool to refer to all year. As she discusses self-questioning, she draws attention to the chart as her students suggest examples for selected categories: Driving Questions (I wonder? How? Why?), Lines from Text (interesting facts, inspiring ideas), and Answers to Questions (Now I realize, I am thinking). When they finish, Lesley moves this class anchor to a small-group setting as other students work independently. This allows all students to immediately apply what they learned in another context. A revised small-group form matches the class anchor chart and students add their sticky note questions to refer to later. Lesley leaves the group during a writing activity so she can visit a student working independently for a brief moment.

Final Reflection

The small changes Lesley made elevated the second lesson sequence. Just ten minutes was needed to complete the whole-class anchor chart, but this saved time and allowed students to apply their learning in other settings. The anchor chart offers a visual reference of learning using a variety of contexts and texts with valuable information that is supplemented with a growing list of examples. Students can then add sticky-note questions

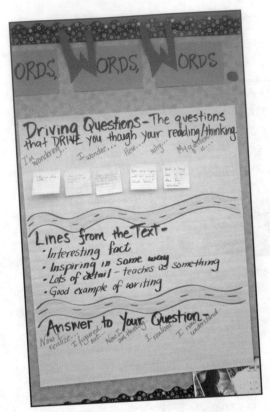

FIGURE 1.10 **Meaningful dialogue offers students and teachers valuable feedback**

FIGURE 1.9 **An interactive anchor chart creates a concrete reference for learning**

FIGURE 1.11 **Lesley assumes a supportive role to address confusions and ensure success**

during small-group learning or as a segue to independent reading. Students then return to a whole-class setting to share or add questions they generated during these varied learning experiences. Through these two lesson sequences, Lesley discovered that great work often occurs through seemingly minor changes. Lesley's enthusiasm and her engaged participation elevated students' learning because she assumed an active role in whole-class, small-group, and independent work. This role is evident in both lesson sequences, but drawing her attention to this increased her awareness so she will be more intentional in the future. Lesley is now more mindful of her critical role in the learning process and she is doing more great work as a result.

Based on our discussion, Lesley revised her students' form to match the anchor chart. Often, we must acknowledge that doing less in more effective ways can enhance our instruction. Lesley can reflect on the minor but significant changes needed for more focused instructional experiences that lead to deeper levels of understanding. If our end goal is to maximize their comprehension, this is certainly an idea worth considering.

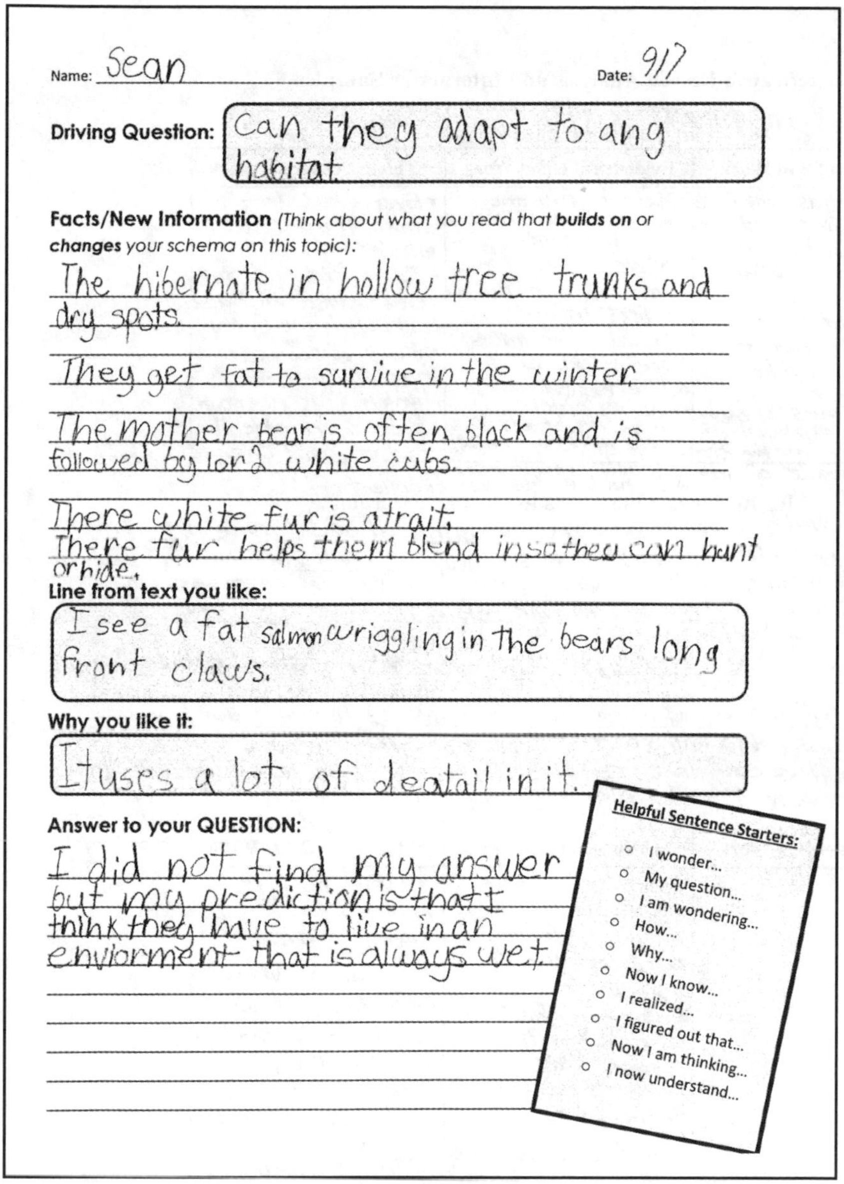

Name: Sean

Date: 9/7

Driving Question: Can they adapt to any habitat

Facts/New Information *(Think about what you read that **builds on** or **changes** your schema on this topic):*

The hibernate in hollow tree trunks and dry spots.

They get fat to survive in the winter.

The mother bear is often black and is followed by 1 or 2 white cubs.

There white fur is a trait.
There fur helps them blend in so they can hunt or hide.

Line from text you like:

I see a fat salmon wriggling in the bears long front claws.

Why you like it:

I uses a lot of deatail in it.

Answer to your QUESTION:

I did not find my answer but my prediction is that I think they have to live in an enviorment that is always wet.

Helpful Sentence Starters:
- I wonder...
- My question...
- I am wondering...
- How...
- Why...
- Now I know...
- I realized...
- I figured out that...
- Now I am thinking...
- I now understand...

FIGURE 1.12 **The open-ended form makes a connection to the class anchor chart goals**

I asked Lesley to explore this process using our Reflective Lesson Analysis and Interactive Samples form. This completed form allows us to see what achieving more great work is all about through Lesley's eyes. Her initial teaching is a lens for viewing and adjusting the second teaching sequence. Lesley shows us what is possible when we closely examine our own practices and then make the necessary changes to elevate those practices. The form makes this reflective process concrete and visible.

Reflective Lesson Analysis and Interactive Samples

Initial Instructional Activity

Evidence of Bad Work	Evidence of Good Work	Evidence of Great Work
• Not all kids who were Ind. Reading read the whole time – I want every minute to count for all kids. • Kids did not have an an anchor to us- to refer to when working. • First 5 mins. of each group is explaining task + teaching the form- is this a waste of time?	• Many kids in the classroom were reading the whole time. • Kids in small group read and responded to text in writing. • Used high interest nonfiction text • I created a graphic organizer (thinking sheet) to help kids organize, share + recall thinking. • I had a place vocab collection.	• Every kid in the small group read the whole time • Each kid got to read aloud (and discuss text) with me (1:1 whisper read) • Kids discussed + shared questions + thinking as a group. • Kids were able to add to and change schema.

Instructional Adjustments to Maximize learning

➤ I will teach vocabulary collecting at a separate time/day.

➤ When kids are working in sm. group I will take a few moments to roam and check in with others (prob. ½ way through sm. group).

➤ I will create an anchor chart that is interactive and reuseable.

➤ I will add sentence starters to thinking sheet + anchor chart.

➤ I will do a mini-lesson (whole group) to teach the form to the class (this will spare 5+ mins. from each group).

➤ For less confident readers I will us the lower level NG mag.

➤ Next time I will record 3-5 imp. details @ the end of day #1 to remind kids at the start of day #2.

Follow-Up Instructional Activity

Evidence of Bad Work	Evidence of Good Work	Evidence of Great Work
	• used high interest nonfiction (still need to get different levels of the same mag.) • anchor chart was interactive + helped kids understand what to do and how	• every minute counted for Ind. Readers + small group! • Small group was engaged in discussion and very interested in the text • All kids succeeded – it was not too hard/easy for any.
	• Sent. starters on the chart helped kids to be successful	• The streamlined thinking sheet made it easy for kids to know what to do. • All kids knew what to do b/c of short whole group mini-lesson

FIGURE 1.13 **Lesley identifies changes that will move her closer to great work**

Two of Lesley's colleagues will use the same reflective process to broaden your view by examining varied grades and settings in action. Let's begin with first-grade teacher Simone Austin, who has taught for fourteen years. Lesley modeled our first form but you can experience this thoughtful process by completing the form with us this time.

SPOTLIGHT TEACHER

Simone Austin, Grade 1: Initial Teaching Sequence

As I enter the room, three first-grade students are gathered around the table. Simone gives them a book she selected at their independent level. They briefly review words on index cards. Simone begins the lesson by modeling a book talk using a previous read-aloud so she can share familiar events. Simone emphasizes that a book talk does not tell everything and explains how she decided what to share. She then asks the students to whisper-read on their own as she rotates to listen. When one child reads silently, she reminds her to whisper-read. She repeats this reminder on two occasions. Two of the students finish early and quietly wait for the other to finish. After they read, each child does a book talk using their personal text. Simone compliments their efforts and asks probing questions if they falter ("That's a good connection to the skates. Do you have skates?"). Her positive approach helps students share as she uses their ideas as models ("How did Abby help us get to know her book?"). Her supportive demeanor in this very small setting will lead to more detailed book talks in the future.

Now use the form to record what you feel may represent bad work, good work, or great work at the top and instructional adjustments she can make in the center. When you finish writing, compare your notes with our debriefing session.

Debriefing Session

Simone knows comprehension is a critical component of her teaching and she uses read-aloud to model common language for meaningful book talk conversations. Her small groups then help students move beyond trivial details and connect to texts both emotionally and academically. As she reflects on her lesson, Simone identifies several things she may want to eliminate or adjust to elevate her next lesson sequence.

- Use familiar selections such as independent texts or those previously introduced in guided reading. This makes book talks the primary focus.
- Decrease the duration of groups. Ten to fifteen minutes of intense focus can maximize her lesson.

- Encourage silent reading when students are ready. Check for understanding while rotating to discuss the reading with individual children.
- Create a book talk menu as a helpful visual tool. Add discussion points to this supportive anchor reference. Withdraw this support when it is no longer needed.

Follow-Up Teaching Sequence

Students sit at the table with familiar texts. A book talk menu is displayed with three sharing options in the form of questions (What is the character doing? What is the character like? What does the character remind me of?). Simone begins the lesson by reviewing the menu, reminding students to use the chart if they aren't sure what to share. Simone models how to do this with her book. Next students reread to find something about the character they want to share as Simone rotates. These familiar texts allow her to focus on book talks. Simone intentionally addresses words in context, but maintains her purpose. When a child reads silently, she encourages this switch and informally checks for understanding. Simone encourages students to refer to the book while stating ideas in their own words ("What did it say in the book?" "How else can you say that?").

Final Reflection

Simone made small changes that will enhance her book talks. Familiar texts maintain her purpose and the book talk menu offers a supportive scaffold. A narrowed emphasis on characters respects these early stages and allows her to gradually initiate new discussion points. Simone can add to the menu, refer to it during whole-class book talks, or withdraw it as appropriate. She interacts with her students through engaging conversations to

FIGURE 1.14 **Simone uses each moment to teach, reinforce, or support students**

FIGURE 1.15 **A book talk menu offers a concrete tool for informal discussion**

FIGURE 1.16 **Independent and peer-supported applications are used to generate a common language to discuss books**

support her purpose or reinforce learning as those teachable moments arise within the learning activity. She encourages students who are ready for silent reading, using dialogue to increase accountability. These things elevate the quality of her lesson and her students' success. Simone has high expectations for meaningful dialogue in pleasurable contexts for her young readers and she actively models and teaches these expectations. The book talk menu also creates a bridge between home and school.

Completing the form will help Simone consider bad work she can change and good work or great work she can continue or add. Simone takes responsibility for her choices by completing the form and makes changes that will maximize student learning.

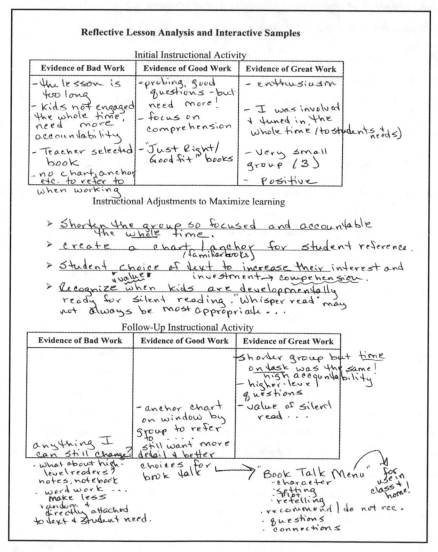

FIGURE 1.17 **Simone reflects on her own teaching to enhance the quality of her instruction to move closer to great work**

Notice that Simone generated a question at the bottom of her form that she will use to guide her teaching in the future. The form initiates the change process but it is designed for her repeated use since she can continue to evaluate her work as she makes new adjustments. I asked Simone to reflect on the changes in these teaching sequences.

The biggest thing I took away was to make every minute count and that I can shorten my groups. Thirty minutes with six-year-olds doing good work is now fifteen minutes of great, high-accountability work. They're getting more out of it. Now I address words in texts so my word work is less random. I love whisper-reading and teacher tune-in so they're accountable and reading the whole time. I've definitely changed my thinking on silent reading and I let them take the lead. It's apparent when they are ready to do that. I especially love the book talk menu and students use it all day and at home.

Now let's meet fifth-grade teacher Danielle King who has taught for four years. Danielle will do a one-to-one lesson with a delightfully capable special education student because "I want to know how to support him as a reader." She knows our most tangled readers have much to teach us. Once again, use the form to experience our collaboration.

SPOTLIGHT TEACHER **Danielle King**, Grade 5: Initial Teaching Sequence

When I arrive, Cody and Danielle are on opposite sides of the table. Cody has self-selected a humorous book from a series. Danielle gives him a graphic organizer she has labeled "before" and "after" in two columns for predictions. Danielle introduces the graphic organizer and then Cody begins reading orally. She asks questions to initiate any new predictions and they list these on the graphic organizer. The text is clearly too challenging and Cody is visibly frustrated when he comes to tricky words. He perseveres with Danielle's support but still struggles. At one point, Danielle stops and asks him to read a list of words. He continues to stumble over words and reads in a word-by-word fashion. Cody seems to understand the gist of the story in spite of this struggle and he describes events he finds interesting in detail, shows personal insight into characters, and recognizes subtle humor. Cody often laughs when discussing events. They continue to list predictions, but Danielle is more focused on encouraging his thoughtful explanations. The supportive environment leads to lively discussions, although inordinate support is still needed when he reads. As the lesson ends, I tell Cody I enjoyed listening to him read. His response reflects the fragile spirit of some of our readers: "Well, I'm a lower-level reader." I immediately reply, "Actually Cody, you are a reader, not a level, and I'm so impressed with you as a reader." He pauses ever so briefly and smiles.

FIGURE 1.18 **Danielle knows that one-to-one opportunities are critical for her tangled readers**

FIGURE 1.19 **Danielle promotes meaningful reading in a high-success experience**

Record evidence of bad work, good work, or great work you noticed in Danielle's lesson at the top of the form and any instructional adjustments that may elevate her lesson in the center. When you finish, compare your notes with our debriefing session.

Debriefing Session

Danielle supports Cody as a reader in an emotionally engaging lesson. We discussed his perception as a "lower-level reader" because we don't want levels to be a defining factor exacerbated by too-challenging experiences. Self-selected texts address interest, but Danielle must balance this with high-success reading to continuously convey the message of Cody as a reader rather than a level. Emotions weigh heavily into Cody's equation, so we explored how to increase confidence and competence simultaneously.

- Create a more informal and supportive atmosphere by sitting side by side with Cody. This simple seating adjustment sets a positive tone for learning.
- Increase success initially using texts with supportive pictures and less print per page. Cody likes fables, science, and poetry so these are excellent options.
- Help Cody become more strategic through independent problem solving. Fade the support of coaching and prompting to encourage this independence.
- Increase Cody's automaticity of high-frequency words before each lesson. Do this by quickly using word cards, magnetic letters, or cut-up sentences.
- Create an engaging, high-success experience. While a graphic organizer is a helpful tool, it may be counterproductive for Cody at this time.

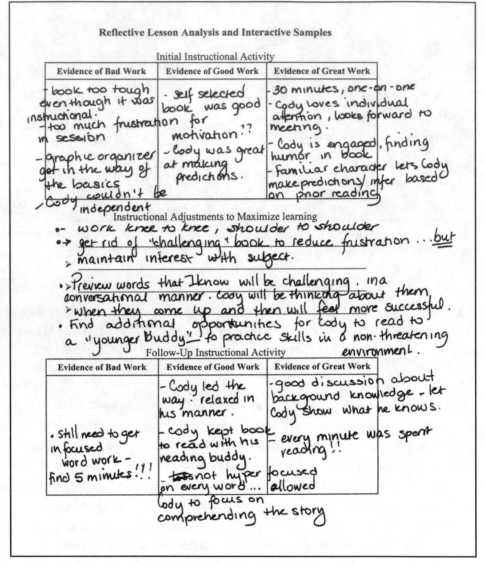

Reflective Lesson Analysis and Interactive Samples

Initial Instructional Activity

Evidence of Bad Work	Evidence of Good Work	Evidence of Great Work
- book too tough even though it was instructional. - too much frustration in session - graphic organizer got in the way of the basics - Cody couldn't be independent	- self selected book was good for motivation?? - Cody was great at making predictions.	- 30 minutes, one-on-one - Cody loves individual attention, looks forward to meeting. - Cody is engaged, finding humor in book - familiar character lets Cody make predictions/infer based on prior reading

Instructional Adjustments to Maximize learning

- work knee to knee, shoulder to shoulder
- → get rid of "challenging" book to reduce frustration... <u>but</u>
  - maintain interest with subject.

- → Preview words that I know will be challenging, in a conversational manner. Cody will be thinking about them, when they come up and then will feel more successful.
- Find additional opportunities for Cody to read to a "younger buddy" to practice skills in a non-threatening environment.

Follow-Up Instructional Activity

Evidence of Bad Work	Evidence of Good Work	Evidence of Great Work
- still need to get in focused word work - find 5 minutes!!!	- Cody led the way. relaxed in his manner. - Cody kept book to read with his reading buddy. - not hyper focused on every word... Cody to focus on comprehending the story	- good discussion about background knowledge - let Cody show what he knows. - every minute was spent reading!! - focused allowed

Follow-Up Teaching Sequence

Cody sits beside Danielle with an African fable he selected. This book has less print per page and supportive illustrations. Cody is noticeably more confident as he reads and Danielle draws attention to pictures to support reading. Their discussions are equally engaging, but he solves problems on his own or with minimal support as Danielle begins to withdraw her support to encourage his growing independence. There is no graphic organizer, placing an emphasis on reading with understanding. Cody makes predictions rising from the discussion but the focus is on the events he finds interesting. His descriptions give Danielle valuable information about Cody as a reader but she lets him lead the way and demonstrates sincere interest in his ideas. Cody is not struggling to read the words and Danielle reinforces his efforts and offers support only as needed. As a result, there is a dramatic difference in Cody's demeanor.

Final Reflection

Danielle views Cody as a capable member of her classroom and she is determined to support him without excuses. Danielle has adopted a sense of urgency by making additional adjustments that will lead to Cody's continued success. Cody enjoys personal time with Danielle, but she can "up the instructional ante" with long-range goals.

- Danielle and the special education teacher need common goals for Cody's continued success. Danielle initiated Leveled Literacy Intervention (grade 2) (2008c) for thirty minutes of daily support and Cody can select his favorite texts to revisit with the special education teacher.
- Cody needs both instructional and independent texts. Danielle asked him to be a buddy for a first grader for independent reading and paired him with a second grader so he can select his favorite instructional texts for familiar reading.
- Danielle created a poetry folder of short humorous poems. This resource is unlimited and Cody can't check reading levels that perpetuate his narrow view.

Danielle's analysis of her work and changes she is making as a result are reflected in her form. This concrete tool highlights these changes and those she still wants to make, such as more focused word work. The form is her road map to increasing expertise.

The thinking that accompanies the form and our reflective conversations lead to a "big win" for Cody. I asked Danielle to reflect on how she now views her work with Cody.

> You saw Cody gets easily discouraged when his reading breaks down. I felt I needed to have him work through every word before moving on, but you said to pick my battles. I'm more sensitive about making this time less frustrating. I'm more careful selecting books and I preview them and support the conversation so he is successful. Since you were here, Cody said to me on several occasions "I am not a level, I am a reader."

These teachers are learning to "pick their battles" by eliminating less effective practices and replacing them with more effective ones. In other words, they are using their own teaching as a pathway to increasing expertise. Imagine where that path may lead as they make additional changes. These changes ultimately benefit their students.

It is important to emphasize that Danielle's choice to use high-success texts is coupled with her goal to close the gap as quickly as possible. She does not view levels as an excuse to sit passively by and maintain the status quo. She uses levels to increase the intensity of her teaching in order to increase that level as soon as possible. Danielle is aware of Cody's changing needs at all times and offers experiences to help him achieve his rightful status as an amazing reader. (And yes, Cody, you *are* an amazing reader!)

A Final Note on Great Work

Great work is the highest level of teaching so it's harder to define. I asked some of the leading minds in literacy to help me define great work and I'll include their thoughts throughout this book. Let's begin with Richard Allington's description based on his exemplary teacher study (Allington 2002; Allington and Johnston 2002):

> *After the kids had departed, our exemplary teachers were usually fired up and looking for someone to listen to them tell a story about something wonderful that happened. After a full day of great work they felt happy and ready to share! When we visited classrooms of "typical" teachers who taught the same grade level in the same school, they seemed tired, worn out, and ready for a nap at the end of the day. If they had a story to tell it was most often about a failure that day. The end of the day for our typical teachers was more "it's finally over." No celebrations or happy talk. After a full day of great work, exemplary teachers are pumped to do more great work with kids tomorrow. (email message to author, June 9, 2011)*

FIGURE 1.21 **Cody is thriving because those who surround him acknowledge his status as an "amazing reader." His fifth-grade teacher, Danielle King, literacy consultant, Mary Howard, and special education teacher, Katie Gioldassis celebrate him as a reader because they know the impact our perception has on Cody's view of himself as a learner.**

Our spotlight teachers are pumped to do more great work, as reflected by their constant stream of emails to me celebrating their successes. They know great work takes place in whole-class, small-group, or one-to-one settings. They know great work is possible each minute of each day because literacy is the thread that permeates the day. Most of all, they know great work is active, meaningful engagement in high-success and enthusiastic literacy for every child, every day (Allington and Gabriel 2012). And that is within the reach of *any* teacher willing to make the commitment to achieve great work. We can and should work to achieve great work for every child, every day. They deserve nothing less!

My personal great work journey began August 1972. At times, I'm elated by the sheer heights of my desire to achieve great work and yet bad work still beckons. But each inevitable bad work moment is a learning opportunity. Bad work today can be our good work or great work tomorrow if we adhere to Stanier's Great Work Truth #3 (2008, 18):

FIGURE 1.22 **Yes, Cody, you *are* an amazing reader!**

> *To do more great work, you need to make not one but two choices.*
>
> *What will you say yes to?*
>
> *What will you say no to?*

Great work requires holding onto good ideas in a time of bad ones (Newkirk 2009). But first, we must distinguish between good ideas and bad ideas and elevate good ideas to great ideas. There are many things you can't control, but you can control the quality of your work in the confines of your classroom. In the next chapter, dedicated teachers taking control will help us explore principles to awaken great work, strategies to support great work, and values that lay a foundation for great work. So our journey continues . . .

CHAPTER 2

Generating Vision Statements and Overarching Goals to Guide Our Literacy Design

> " *Great work springs from clear instructional goals and the belief that all learners can and should be operating at a maximum level of collaboration, engagement and language use in which learning floats on a sea of talk.*"
>
> (Linda Hoyt, email message to author, September 22, 2011)

I had long dreamed of a private floral haven in which to savor life's quiet moments. When my new landscaper arrived, rapid-fire questions drew blank stares. Luckily, he put me out of my misery by asking, "What do you want your garden to say about you?" While the complexities of gardens escape me, I possess an endless store of wisdom reflected in my enthusiastic response. This wise young man allowed me to articulate my vision so we could explore the possibilities together—and my dream became a reality.

Our ability to begin doing the work that matters is based on the same principle. We need the freedom to articulate our vision so that we can explore the possibilities that will become an instructional reality. We thoughtfully shape vision into practice when we are clear about who we are, what we stand for, and what matters to us (Stanier 2010).

In this chapter, we will generate important guidelines with our personal vision and overarching goals. This isn't a soon-forgotten "to-do" list, but an instructional compass to guide our efforts. Short-term goals will help us to "achieve and celebrate a continuous succession of small, quick victories in vital areas." (Schmoker 2004, 427). These goals vary according to *your* students and *your* learning journey. Where do *you* begin? Where do *you* need to go? We need a sense of direction to successfully set and meet our goals.

Overarching components of an effective literacy design offer this sense of direction. Our instructional template reflects the areas we will explore in this book.

Simply put, our instructional design includes active engagement in meaningful, purposeful literacy across the curriculum (listening, speaking, reading, writing); daily activities to inform teaching (ongoing assessment); inviting spaces that nurture literacy (environment); flexible structures in varied settings (organization); quality resources to support and reinforce literacy; and a willingness to create a positive culture that will help students view literacy as a pleasurable pursuit (motivation).

Our instructional design must be based on the highest standards of "best practice." To accomplish this we need a clear, concise definition that will help us to analyze our instructional choices. In this book, *best practice* will be defined as "serious, thoughtful, informed, responsible, state-of-the-art teaching" (Zemelman, Daniels, and Hyde 2012, 2).

FIGURE 2.1 **Overarching Components of an Effective Literacy Design**

This means that we *all* assume 100 percent responsibility for the outcome of our teaching. There is simply no one to blame if we do not achieve the desired outcome—student success. This is possible only when knowledgeable professionals become responsible decision makers. "In the end it will become clearer that there are no 'proven programs,' just schools in which we find more expert teachers—teachers who need no script to tell them what to do" (Allington 2002, 747).

With a cohesive curriculum planted firmly at the center, we establish our first goal to "massively increase the amount of purposeful reading, writing, and discussion students engage in every day, across the disciplines" (Schmoker 2011b, 68). We want students to "hit the ground running" from the first day of school to "experience high involvement, deep engagement, humor, and trust and come to see that books and writing *are* the be-all and end-all" (Blauman 2011, 3). To do this, we must dramatically increase the volume of reading and writing.

Maintaining an Instructional Sense of Direction that Leads to Best Practice

In this chapter, I will use three related but distinctive terms illustrated in Figure 2.2: *vision statement*, *overarching central goals*, and *interactive application*. Many schools have a vision statement with goals, but interactive application is often the missing ingredient that moves us from good ideas on paper to excellent ideas in practice.

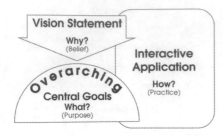

FIGURE 2.2 **Three Factors that Offer an Instructional Sense of Direction**

- Vision Statement (Why?): This reflects our professional beliefs about teaching and learning. Our vision is the heartbeat of the choices we make.
- Overarching Central Goals (What?): A vision statement leads to our overarching goals. These goals identify what we will do based on our beliefs.
- Interactive Application (How?): Interactive application is the critical component. It reflects our practices, or how we will bring our goals to life where it matters.

These interrelated terms guide our efforts toward greater expertise. Vision statements reflect intent while overarching goals are our purpose. But these are only beautifully worded empty promises until we put them into action through interactive application.

First, Create Your Vision Statement

We begin to identify our vision statements by asking, "What do I value? What do I stand for? What are my non-negotiables?" Our answers reflect our belief system or what we hold dear in our teaching. This is our commitment to devote time and energy in the best ways. Here are some sample vision statements (*your* commitment to *students*).

I Believe Students Need . . .

- ample authentic daily reading and writing experiences
- opportunities to develop thoughtful and engaged literacy
- experiences to develop as independent problem solvers
- explicit teacher models designed to demonstrate learning
- gradually faded support through shared and guided practice
- high-success texts that reflect reading level over grade level
- choice in the form of self-selected high-interest texts
- small-group experiences that are flexible and fluid in nature
- side-by-side opportunities to engage with the teacher
- rich collaborations with peers in active experiences
- written references that clearly state learning expectations
- assessments that view students from varied perspectives
- experiences that promote literacy across the curriculum
- a teacher committed to a student-based differentiated stance
- opportunities to develop as enthusiastic and lifelong learners

A vision statement is worthless unless we believe in and abide by the sentiments. When we are fully committed to these, it's much harder to veer from them as we translate our vision into instructional practices. Start small with one vision statement you truly value and concentrate your energy and time to achieving that one thing.

Next, Translate Your Vision Statement into Overarching Central Goals

Now we translate these vision statements into overarching central goals. These will serve as an instructional guide—what we will do to put that vision into action. As shown in this example, our goals detail how we will move from a belief to a specific purpose.

Vision Statement: I believe students need small-group experiences that are flexible and fluid in nature. I can achieve this goal by doing the following:

- model learning goals in a whole-class focus lesson to introduce a skill or strategy
- create anchor charts to highlight learning goals in varied contexts
- initiate homogeneous instructional groups based on current reading levels
- alternate heterogeneous groups using independent texts to reinforce learning
- change group membership according to purpose or intent for flexibility
- emphasize silent reading while using oral reading to support key ideas
- initiate assessments that explore students' ability to discuss important ideas
- use simple open-ended reference tools to record key ideas
- revisit key learning points in a whole-group setting and add to anchor charts

Finally, Determine the Interactive Application that Reflects Your Teaching Practices

We make our goals interactive by defining how we will apply them in practice. This essential component to goal setting focuses on the quality of our work. Our vision statements and goals help us consider what we want to achieve, determine roadblocks that stand in our way to achieving those things (bad work), and focus on practices that will heighten our work (good/great work). Honest reflection and careful planning are central to achieving great work.

Putting Our Goals into Action

Let's begin this interactive process with our first form in the chapter. The Ongoing Goal Setting Pie Chart is a personal glimpse of your work to uncover areas that may need attention. Start with one area (such as small-group reading activities) to devote your energy to a specific goal and collaborate with those who have the same goal.

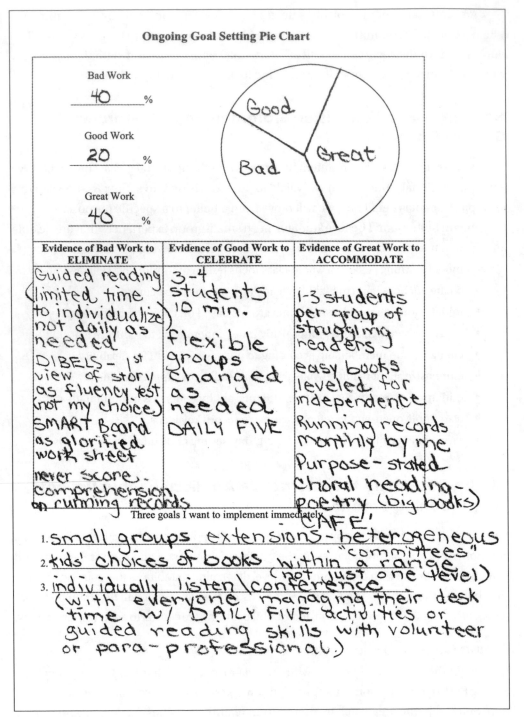

Ongoing Goal Setting Pie Chart

Bad Work

40 %

Good Work

20 %

Great Work

40 %

Evidence of Bad Work to ELIMINATE	Evidence of Good Work to CELEBRATE	Evidence of Great Work to ACCOMMODATE
Guided reading (limited time to individualize not daily as needed) DIBELS - 1st view of story as fluency test (not my choice) SMART board as glorified work sheet never score comprehension on running records	3-4 students 10 min. flexible groups changed as needed DAILY FIVE	1-3 students per group of struggling readers easy books leveled for independence Running records monthly by me Purpose - stated choral reading - poetry (big books) CAFE'

Three goals I want to implement immediately

1. small groups extensions - heterogeneous
   "committees"
2. kids' choices of books within a range (not just one level)
3. individually listen\conference (with everyone managing their desk time w/ DAILY FIVE activities or guided reading skills with volunteer or para-professional)

FIGURE 2.3 **Sharon honestly reflects on her teaching in order to move closer to great work**

First-grade teacher Sharon Davis, from Sunset Terrace Elementary in Rochester, Minnesota, uses our form to make her goals visible. After twenty-five years of teaching, Sharon knows there is always room to grow. The form reflects these growth opportunities and puts bad work, good work, and great work in clear view so that ineffective practices can be substituted for those that are more likely to increase the quality of her teaching.

Sharon identifies potential bad work of sporadic small groups, limited individual support, the limitation of DIBELS, using SMART Board ineffectively, and a narrowed view of running records. She celebrates

FIGURE 2.4 **Sharon learns a great deal about her students by observing them as they actively engage in learning**

varied small groups with flexibility, Daily Five (Boushey and Moser 2006), smaller groups for struggling readers, time for independent reading, taking her own running records, and setting a clear purpose for reading.

The form helps Sharon target three things she will implement immediately to achieve her goals. She is elevating small-group and individual work by building her independent library and adding conferences. Putting her plan in writing allows her to adjust her goals as she works to achieve them. Recording her incremental changes in writing helps Sharon articulate how she will accomplish her goals and provides a sense of direction.

As a result, Sharon is offering more individualized support and promoting student independence. She uses daily "committee work" (collaborative groups) in small-group experiences to rotate and support their efforts or work with individuals or small groups. Sharon is making active engagement in literacy through varied support opportunities her priority, and she works toward achieving these central goals one day at a time. Small incremental adjustments can set change in motion and become giant leaps.

Sharon is learning that immersion in print is integral to learning—and reading, writing, and talking are becoming her focus. She takes advantage of teachable moments and uses more teacher and cocreated anchor charts and student-initiated writing. Sharon explains how these initial changes are impacting her teaching:

> In every way! I used to think I needed permission to do things I know my kids need but now I give myself permission. They work in committees (collaborative groups) every day because I know they need to talk and work things out on their own. I rotate to learn more about them or work with individual students. I use anchor charts in just about everything I do so they see me write and see their own thinking. The change? Huge!

FIGURE 2.5 **Teri knows a classroom library will support her goal to initiate small groups**

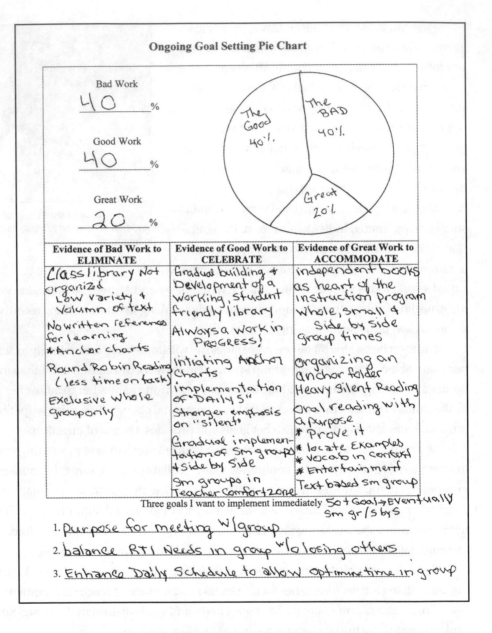

Ongoing Goal Setting Pie Chart

Bad Work

40 %

Good Work

40 %

Great Work

20 %

The Good 40%.
The BAD 40%.
Great 20%.

Evidence of Bad Work to ELIMINATE	Evidence of Good Work to CELEBRATE	Evidence of Great Work to ACCOMMODATE
Class library not organized Low variety + volumn of text No written references for learning *Anchor charts Round Robin Reading (less time on task) Exclusive whole group only	Gradual building + Development of a working, student friendly library Always a work in PROGRESS! Initiating Anchor Charts implementation of "DAILY 5" Stronger emphasis on "silent" Gradual implementation of Sm group + side by side Sm groups in Teacher Comfort zone	independent books as heart of the instruction program whole, small & side by side group times organizing an anchor folder Heavy silent Reading Oral reading with a purpose *Prove it *locate Examples *Vocab in context *Entertainment Text based sm group

Three goals I want to implement immediately So+Goal→Eventually Sm gr/s by S

1. purpose for meeting w/group
2. balance RTI Needs in group w/o losing others
3. Enhance Daily Schedule to allow optimum time in group

Fourth-grade teacher Teri Hood in Mustang, Oklahoma, also completed the form. She identified three big goals: classroom library, oral reading alternatives to round-robin, and flexible small groups. Putting this in writing helps to identify ongoing goals and ensure consistency so the form becomes the instructional glue of her teaching.

It is also helpful to generate a collaborative chart *as long as teachers maintain control of it.* Mustang Elementary administrator Laquita Semmler and reading specialist Jackie

Stafford are working with a teacher volunteer. The chart (seen in Figure 2.6) reflects the bad-good-great continuum with their identified focus of guided reading on the left. They can add new goals according to their needs during the course of the year. The chart gives them a concrete tool for discussion as they visibly work toward their goals.

FIGURE 2.6 **A Bad Work–Good Work–Great Work Chart establishes common goals**

A miniversion of the chart (Figure 2.7) allows teachers to select personal goals. Attach two file folders in the center with the instructional focus in the left column (guided reading) and bad-good-great categories in the remaining columns. Goals are recorded on sticky notes so that the contents of the folder can be individualized.

Now the focus and goals can be easily rearranged, added, or omitted using the sticky notes. Fifth-grade teacher Stephanie Weaver in Mustang, Oklahoma, is adding goals for guided reading by moving the the sticky notes under each category (see Figure 2.8). She can change her goals or her area of focus as her needs change. For example, small groups will be shorter in duration in the early stages as she is building stamina, or the time students can work unsupported while she is with a small group. She will increase her small-group time frames as she offers explicit models and promotes greater independence.

Let's take a closer look at some sample charts. There is no one-size-fits-all view so these vary from school to school or teacher to teacher and are intended to provide a flexible guide for discussion. We may not focus on guided reading if teachers are skilled in

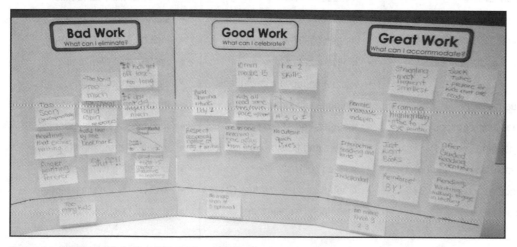

FIGURE 2.7 **Mini Bad Work–Good Work–Great Work Chart**

FIGURE 2.8 **Stephanie personalizes her goals based on her professional needs and the instructional needs of her students**

this area. Ideally, focus on areas you, or teachers in your group, do not feel confident in yet. Of course the chart can also help to clarify an approach to ensure a common and high-quality perspective. The chart should have concrete, instructionally based descriptors.

Charts lead us to explore a common understanding of instructional practices. For example, many teachers are still wedded to round-robin reading, defined as "the outmoded practice of calling on students to read orally one after the other" (Harris and Hodges 1995, 222). Ash, Kuhn, and Walpole note that one-third of teachers they studied use it despite acknowledging it as ineffective (2009). Knowing the research makes it hard to defend this activity, particularly the heavy reliance on oral reading that often occurs with poor readers (Allington and McGill-Franzen 2010).

INSTRUCTIONAL FOCUS: SMALL-GROUP GUIDED READING		
Bad Work	**Good Work**	**Great Work**
What Can We Eliminate?	*What Can We Celebrate?*	*What Can We Accommodate?*
• too many students (6+)	• (small) 3–5 (K smaller)	• size according to need (3–4)
• limited to grade-level texts	• carefully matched texts	• increasing variety/text type
• restricted (chapter/narrative)	• wide range of texts	• includes emphasis expository
• frustration level	• instructional texts	• both instructional/familiar
• one-size-fits-all lesson	• needs-based lesson	• student-based instruction
• too long for attention needs	• ranges 10 (K) to 15/20 min.	• include 5-min. *Quick Takes*
• too many goals to cover	• limited number of goals	• deeper level of meaning
• teacher not engaged	• teacher engaged with students	• student engagement is high
• dialogue is stilted	• dialogue is informal	• thoughtful student dialogue
• questions interrogational	• thoughtful questions posed	• includes student questioning
• static grouping (named)	• flexible and fluid groups	• variety of grouping options
• round-robin/choral reading	• all read softly/silently	• oral reading with a purpose
• oral reading focus grade 2+	• emphasize silent reading (2+)	• explicitly teach silent reading
• worksheet focus	• meaningful experiences	• personal response options

With this understanding, we can initiate conversations to design more effective oral reading practices as well as to consider the critical role of silent reading beyond the earliest grades (Hiebert and Reutzel 2010).

INSTRUCTIONAL FOCUS: ORAL READING PRACTICES		
Bad Work	**Good Work**	**Great Work**
What Can We Eliminate?	*What Can We Celebrate?*	*What Can We Accommodate?*
• focus on oral reading	• oral reading with a purpose	• oral reading to support text
• round-robin reading	• students read softly or silently	• teacher listening to individuals
• unrehearsed public reading	• rehearsed reading for sharing	• time to practice
• oral reading of frustration text	• selected reading after support	• student-selected texts
• teacher-selected text	• student-selected segments	• time to "be the expert"
• one-size-fits-all	• peer collaboration activities	• independent reading activities

The power of these charts is that they help us to initiate deeper discussions. For example, we may discuss purposes for oral reading such as to support thinking or celebrate beautiful language. Charts don't just label ideas, but help set our sights on more effective practices. This may lead to a new chart to reflect what the other students are doing as we work in small groups, as shown in the following instructional focus chart.

INSTRUCTIONAL FOCUS: INDEPENDENT SEATWORK ACTIVITIES		
Bad Work	**Good Work**	**Great Work**
What Can We Eliminate?	*What Can We Celebrate?*	*What Can We Accommodate?*
• unfamiliar learning (teach)	• familiar (extend learning)	• independent application
• too hard and frustrating	• reinforcing	• varied contexts
• passive worksheets	• open-ended thinking forms	• integration of reading/writing
• trivial "stuff"	• reading and writing focus	• include meaningful peer talk
• assigned tasks	• build in options	• student-suggested options
• simply a grade	• offer feedback	• include peer feedback
• one-size-fits-all books	• use of independent texts	• include wider variety
• teacher at the desk	• teacher with students	• time to rotate or confer
• begin too soon	• explicitly teach rituals	• revisit over time

FIGURE 2.9 **Teachers use minicharts to work toward common goals**

The charts reflect our discussion about what students do or do not do. They offer a flexible interactive tool for discussion, helping us to identify where we are at that time and changing as our instructional goals change.

Mustang Elementary School first-grade teachers Nicole Erwin and Gayla Holmes work with kindergarten teacher Jamie Khosravi on an instructional chart. They are creating a personal working tool to move instructional goals into classroom practice through collaboration. Imagine the value of discussions arising from sharing goals and expectations across grade levels.

A distinctive feature of this interactive process is that we move from *intent* (vision) and *purpose* (overarching goals) to *action* (interactive application). Too often, goals are well intentioned but vague or they tell teachers to *do* something with no explanation *how* to accomplish it in the most effective ways. We put our goals in writing and break them down into instructionally specific terms so that we can be very clear as we describe how we will apply them in a learning setting. This is central to great work.

Putting Professional Decision Making and Planning into Perspective

We have looked at a three-step process for establishing concrete instructional goals. This is *not* an obligatory checklist, but a thoughtful design grounded in purposeful intent. Worthy goals don't sidetrack us with irrelevant issues like raising test scores. They are a "moral purpose" based on increasing student learning (Fullan 2002; Fullan, Bertani, and Quinn 2004). We can never lose sight of the fact that student success is our job!

I'd be remiss if I don't emphasize that supportive professional collaborations will intensify this process (Gabriel, Day, and Allington 2011). Dialogue can deepen our understanding and avoids "instructional perseveration," or repeating ineffective strategies year after year (Applegate, Applegate, and Turner 2010). Committing our goals to paper leads to "relentless consistency" so our actions are motivated by common principles (Fullan 2008).

The spotlight teachers in this chapter began their transition by identifying one big goal on the chart to work toward all year. Concrete written references help them identify and translate that goal into action as a "touchstone" to shape their practices in the future (Turner, Applegate, and Applegate 2011). In other words, their teaching will be forever influenced by these big goals because they were selected thoughtfully.

Let's begin with Katie Gioldassis, a special education teacher in Sunapee, New Hampshire. Katie has taught for three years and was a paraeducator, substitute, and volunteer for several years prior. Katie will demonstrate our next form to break down a central goal by identifying the action steps that will help her achieve that goal.

SPOTLIGHT TEACHER **Katie Gioldassis**, Special Education: Initial Teaching Observation

I enter Katie's special education room and see two fifth-grade students reading on their own as Katie watches. She explains that students read independently from a book of their choice for the first few minutes of each session. When they finish reading, she gives them a nonfiction book about trains. After explaining that nonfiction books are written to teach something and give us information, they turn to the glossary (which she compares to a minidictionary). She poses questions about how this can help readers and they discuss several words. This preview takes about five minutes of small-group time. She reminds them to use prior knowledge as they read. They begin reading orally by taking turns as the other follows along. If a student has difficulty with a word, she helps them break it apart (*engine, commuter*). Students appear visibly restless when they wait for their turn. When they finish reading, she initiates an informal dialogue about the topic and draws attention to several effective strategies she noticed.

Debriefing Session

Katie did many outstanding things including time for independent reading; inclusion of informational texts; noticing and referencing strategies; and drawing attention to new or important ideas, words, or concepts. She clearly wants students to be successful and she does many things to achieve this goal. We must always begin with the wonderful things we are already doing while considering what to alter in the future. I *never* use the term "bad work." Rather, I help teachers consider changes they can make that will increase the quality of their instruction. Our discussion began as Katie took ownership of her teaching: "I talk too much and I think my students need to do more talking." Her evidence of bad work does not make Katie a "bad" teacher, but helps her recognize changes that can lead to increasingly skilled teaching. At least in part, this is due to her school's emphasis on professional development within a respectful dialogue.

During our discussion, we identified some simple adjustments Katie can make.

- Incorporate familiar reading of previous texts for independent reading time. This accommodates choice but offers repetition of past reading material.

Interactive Central Goal with a Working Action Plan

Targeted Central Goal		Ongoing Reflections
-Promote independent problem solving through instructional support and guided practice in small groups.		

Goal Date	Working Action Steps to Achieve the Central Goal	Ongoing Reflections
9/30/11	※ -Begin with independent/familiar text and establish purpose before reading.	Writing purpose on the board is a good reminder.
9/30/11	※ -Use of high-interest informational	
10/31/11	-let students talk more by asking questions.	
11/30/11	-Tell students what I notice in terms of strategies.	
9/30/11	※ -Create an anchor chart to provide visual/show what students are learning	Refer to anchor chart when you estab. purpose.
9/30/11	※ -Use sticky notes to organize thinking on a chart.	Students prefer the lined sticky notes.
9/30/11	※ -let students read silently as I tap in/help individual students.	Observe also for whisper reading vs. silent reading
11/30/11	-Only read small parts orally to help/enhance the discussion.	

FIGURE 2.10 **Katie reflects on specific steps to work toward her goals according to a personal timeline**

- Take advantage of this time by conferring briefly with students as they read or listen to small portions. This is a chance to spend one-to-one time with students.

- Set a clear purpose for reading and revisit it often. Displaying the purpose in writing helps students establish and meet their reading purpose and goals.

- Avoid getting sidetracked by taking too long to address the glossary or index. Creating a features chart to refer to later may be a future lesson focus.

- Use silent reading to increase student engagement. Oral reading can be used to reinforce the reading or to check for understanding as you rotate.

- Pose probing questions to support meaning and make students accountable: How do you know? What did it say? Give me an example. Where did you read that?

- Avoid relying too heavily on the visual features of reading, making sure to emphasize meaning and reinforce comprehension often. (Did that make sense? What made this confusing? What did you do to understand your reading?)

- Create a written reference to organize students' thinking in the form of a graphic organizer or anchor chart. This can be used to highlight key ideas and as a tool to support meaningful collaborations about the reading experience.

Our discussion helps Katie use her central goal to initiate change with our form (see Figure 2.10). Interactive Central Goal with a Working Action Plan gives Katie an ongoing reference for identifying action steps to accomplish her goal within a specific time frame.

Final Reflection

The difference in Katie as she is working toward these goals is dramatic. Her students are more engaged because she sets a clear purpose in writing, focuses on silent reading with purposeful oral reading, uses anchor chart references, and rotates as students read. But the most dramatic change is Katie's newfound awareness of choices that impact her students' potential for success. In the end, our success is measured by their success so this realization is worth celebrating.

The changes Katie has made and continues to make are not due to mandates, scripts, or being made to feel she is not the teacher she clearly wants to be. Great work is within reach regardless of the support or experience we may have. We create the vision that we alone can turn into reality. By identifying evidence of her own bad work and considering how to move closer to great work, Katie altered her own reality, as reflected in her words:

FIGURE 2.11 **Katie engages students in learning both academically and emotionally**

I'm evolving in terms of my effectiveness with my students! I'm more self-aware of how my teaching impacts my students in developing as independent, successful readers, not just decoders. They are internalizing strategies to achieve deeper thinking in comprehension and they are becoming much more confident readers. It is a joy to watch them mature as they grow as readers. (Katie Gioldassis, email message to author, September 21, 2011)

Now we'll travel to Sunset Terrace Elementary in Rochester, Minnesota, to see how two fourth-grade teachers are working toward long-term goals. This time, you will see the discussion occur first so the teachers can apply what they learned from our discussion in the lesson that follows. These teachers will use the same form, giving you two more viewpoints. Please join our conversations once again as you use the form.

 SPOTLIGHT TEACHER

Melinda Holtegaard, Grade 4:
Pre-Lesson Discussion

FIGURE 2.12 **Supportive dialogue helps Melinda verbalize her working goals**

Melinda Holtegaard has taught for fourteen years. Melinda begins by identifying her central goal of literature groups. She has selected the working action steps from our bad-good-great chart to achieve this, including eliminate round-robin reading, set a clear purpose for reading, and emphasize silent reading. Melinda explains that these thirty-minute sessions revolve around chapter books she selects at their reading level, that her instructional purpose changes according to her goals, and that she created a packet of response sheets students complete. This is a starting point to explore her action steps.

- A long-term display to set a clear purpose will provide a visible reminder to stay on track. To make it more interactive, she can use removable cards to display her changing purpose on the chart according to the lesson goals.

- Since her goal is to create more meaningful literature groups, reading and talking should be the focus of the learning activities. To accomplish this, she may want to increase the allotted time of thirty minutes.

- She can make discussions more text based by letting students record their ideas on sticky notes rather than simply completing a response packet. They can do this as they read on their own or in groups as a reference of their thinking.

FIGURE 2.13 **Melinda introduces a common learning goal in a whole-class lesson**

Initial Lesson Based on Our Discussion

As I enter the room, students sit on the floor around Melinda in a gathering area. Melinda introduces her new interactive chart and draws attention to the words *author's purpose* printed on a card. She explains the chart will display the purpose so they won't lose track of their discussion goal. She reviews today's goal and reminds them to "prove" their thinking with text examples. Melinda maintains this purpose while taking advantage of opportunities that arise ("That's a wonderful prediction. Did your thinking change?" "We talked about summarizing last week. How will that help you as a reader?"). She then asks students to take turns reading their written summary in the packet from the previous day. Next, students form small groups and continue reading and discussing. They stop to record their thinking on the sticky notes with peers or on their own. Melinda rotates during small-group and independent activities, observing or talking with students.

Final Reflection and Future Recommendations

Melinda creates an engaging literacy experience as she works toward her action steps. By having students gather around her on the floor, she is able to create a sense of community in an informal atmosphere that supports their conversations. The interactive chart helps her establish her purpose for more focused instruction. We discuss

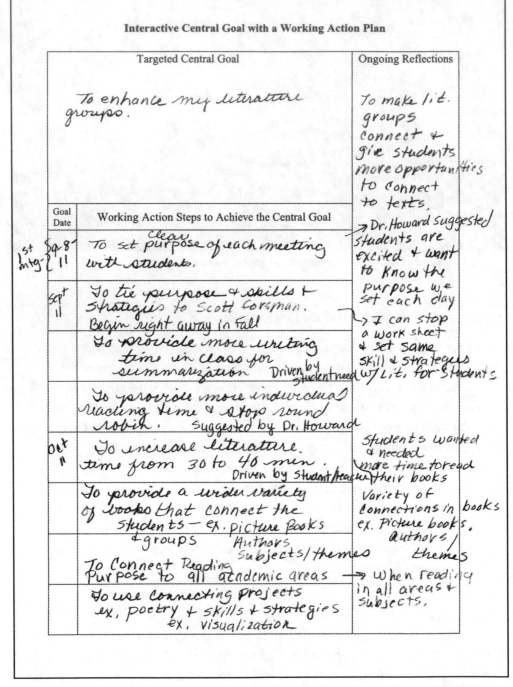

Interactive Central Goal with a Working Action Plan

Targeted Central Goal		Ongoing Reflections
To enhance my literature groups.		To make lit. groups connect & give students more opportunities to connect to texts.

Goal Date	Working Action Steps to Achieve the Central Goal	Ongoing Reflections
1st mtg Sep 8 '11	To set clear purpose of each meeting with students.	→ Dr. Howard suggested students are excited & want to know the purpose we set each day
Sept 11	To tie purpose & skills & strategies to Scott Foresman. Begin right away in Fall	→ I can stop a work sheet & set same skill & strategies w/ Lit. for students
	To provide more writing time in class for summarization Driven by student need	
	To provide more individual reading time & stops round robin. Suggested by Dr. Howard	
Oct 11	To increase literature time from 30 to 40 min. Driven by Student/Teacher	Students wanted & needed more time to read their books
	To provide a wider variety of books that connect the students — ex. picture Books & groups Authors Subjects/themes	Variety of connections in books ex. Picture books. Authors/ themes
	To Connect Reading Purpose to all academic areas →	When reading in all areas & subjects.
	To use connecting projects ex. poetry & skills & strategies ex. visualization	

FIGURE 2.14 **Melinda establishes goals she will personalize according to the learning needs of her students**

new action steps she can initiate as she is ready for "big" possibilities in the future. Melinda knows there is always room to grow so she organizes these accordingly.

- Add ten more minutes for literature groups to incorporate new goals. This gives students more time to read and achieve deeper levels of understanding.

- Add picture books, poetry, and content area selections to broaden goals. Students need varied experiences in addition to chapter books.

- Explicitly teach students to choose "just-right books" (Boushey and Moser 2006) and move to student-selected texts. At some point, we need to trust students to make good choices once we establish supportive guidelines.

- Maximize discussion with more "turn and talk." This will allow Melinda to listen in on conversations as students share their own ideas or those of others.

- Use forms selectively to focus on the main goal. The addition of sticky notes may be more valuable than some of the current recording worksheets.

Look at Melinda's form where she identifies a relevant targeted central goal to elevate her literature groups (see Figure 2.14). Her reflection in the sidebar of the form is compelling and reflects her commitment to students: "Students wanted and needed more time to read." If student learning is our first priority, shouldn't our choices revolve around their needs?

Now let's visit Melinda's colleague, Barb Basse, to see how she addresses her central goal. Use the form to consider what you might discuss with Barb.

SPOTLIGHT TEACHER **Barb Basse**, Grade 4: Pre-Lesson Discussion

Barb Basse has taught for eighteen years but she still struggles with a common challenge that can stymie our efforts to teach effectively—too many goals. Barb came to our session armed with stacks of materials and no clear focus. Our first goal was to increase her instructional power by identifying more focused goals. Barb's targeted central goal is to increase the effectiveness of small-group instruction, so our discussion explored working action steps to help her as she is moving toward this worthy goal.

- Teach for deeper understanding. Having a specific focus will allow her to initiate shorter, more frequent small groups.

- Use this time to build strategic knowledge. She can integrate her whole-class comprehension goals with the goals she is working toward in flexible groups.

- Incorporate more content area texts, such as newsmagazines. She can easily achieve this goal with these high-interest selections.

- Emphasize silent reading. Barb can rotate to listen to students read brief portions without sacrificing this important goal.

- Use sticky notes so students can record their thinking according to the purpose of the lesson. These can then be used to support their discussions.
- Create anchor charts to give students a visual reference of the strategies they are learning. This reinforces that learning and initiates new discussions.

FIGURE 2.15 **Barb gradually initiates learning goals through shared learning collaborations**

Barb and I then taught a small-group lesson together to provide a shared model for her action steps. Barb selected three students and a news-magazine on snakes and we worked together to create an open-ended anchor chart for this small-group lesson. Our anchor chart included three sections: generate questions before reading, respond to questions during reading, and summarize learning after reading. We covered the print with sticky notes for students to generate logical questions based on available preview information rather than random guesses. Then they removed the sticky notes and read silently to respond to those questions or generate new ones.

We then discussed and organized the new sticky notes on the chart. Barb made observations based on her knowledge of her students. These astute observations and a supportive model helped her envision more focused strategy groups. Coplanning and coteaching are an outstanding way to move toward our action steps.

Pause for a moment and think about what you might discuss with Barb or how her learning can support your teaching. Then read to see how Barb applies her new goals.

Initial Lesson Based on Our Discussion and Shared Teaching Experience

As I enter the room, I see each student in Barb's fourth-grade class actively engaged in learning. She just taught a whole-class lesson on fact and opinion so students are now working on that goal independently, with peers or in small groups. Four students sit at the table with a book about whales. Barb creates a jigsaw lesson by letting them choose a section of interest and read to find their "best facts" to share with the group. As they read silently, Barb reads her own copy and records her facts. Students write their selected fact on a sticky note as Barb continues to work on her own. Some students finish early and wait for the others. Each student shares an idea and puts it on a small chart labeled "fact" and "opinion." After they discuss their chosen fact, she asks them to turn that fact into an opinion to show the distinction. Most students do this easily after she shares her example, although it's more challenging for one student. Barb supports him as others wait. After reading, they revisit their learning using the chart.

Final Reflection and Future Recommendations

Planning and implementing a small-group lesson together gave Barb confidence to do this lesson on her own. Based on Barb's selected goals, we discussed further action steps she can add to her form. Goal setting is not a one-shot proposition but an ongoing effort. She will continuously revisit the form and adjust her goals accordingly.

- Explicitly model first, and then rotate as students read. This on-the-spot support will be more valuable than reading on her own as students work.

- Give students something to think about to alleviate wait time while rotating. For example, ask them to reread the text or add more details to a sticky note.

- Model how to find information and then restate it in one's own words. This will ensure understanding by interpreting ideas rather than merely citing them.

- Make groups more flexible by varying them every few weeks. We must ensure that group memberships are not viewed as permanent assignments.

Now look at Barb's form (Figure 2.17). Consider how the instructional adjustments she made in this lesson elevated her teaching and will offer a springboard to additional adjustments.

Barb has launched a new instructional course. She no longer tries to accomplish too much in one lesson, uses anchor charts and sticky notes consistently, emphasizes silent over oral reading, and rotates for more purposeful engagement. She is fine-tuning her central goal of more effective small groups and regularly reflects on and adjusts her action steps. Barb's confidence and expertise are growing with her renewed commitment.

FIGURE 2.16 **Barb fine-tunes her goals as she gains new understandings in the context of her own teaching**

Interactive Central Goal with a Working Action Plan

Targeted Central Goal	Ongoing Reflections
Increase the effectiveness of my small group instruction based on the common goals.	

Goal Date	Working Action Steps to Achieve the Central Goal	
10/31 "	Begin with nonfiction articles to model questioning to set purpose for reading.	– Write sample questions
10/31 "	Use of sticky notes to engage students and track their thinking.	
10/27 "	Create flexible groups by adjusting groupings by need not by specific reading levels.	– groups are constantly changing
11/7 2011	Model a teacher think aloud to set the stage for fact and opinion.	– Whole group first.
11/8	Provide guided practice in finding facts in nonfiction text.	– Write fact on sticky note and post on anchor chart
11/8	Change fact statement to an opinion statement and post next to fact statement on chart	– Model an example
12/9 2011	Require students to read silently with a purpose for reading.	– Give students something to think about while they wait
12/a	Observe students independent practice to assess their knowledge.	– flipbooks made by students

FIGURE 2.17 **Barb reflects on her teaching using a concrete tool that will support her efforts in the future**

Establishing a Sense of Instructional Urgency for Doing the Work that Matters

Our spotlight teachers establish and work toward goals because they are fueled by a "sense of urgency." "With a true sense of urgency, people want to come to work each day ready to cooperate energetically and responsively. . . . And they do" (Kotter 2008, 8). They work toward relevant goals with an inner conviction that says, "Don't tell me why I can't do it. Tell me how I can get it done" (Luntz 2011, 28). This inner conviction drives us to critically evaluate our work and continue to reach for higher levels of excellence.

These teachers have support for their change process, but I am only a conduit for change. Any teacher can be a literacy leader with "commitment, determination, and dedication" (Turner, Applegate, and Applegate 2009, 2011). These teachers changed because they took responsibility for their teaching and used the forms to think more deeply about their instructional choices. You can use the forms to achieve the same remarkable results if you are willing to approach your teaching with the same personal responsibility for your choices. We always have a choice to be the effective teachers our students deserve.

In this chapter, we explored inseparable change features: the vision statement (Why?); the overarching central goals (What?); and the interactive application (How?). A vision statement reflects our beliefs while central goals reflect our purpose. Purpose is "the hinge that everything else hangs upon" (Spence 2009, 10). Purpose offers a sense of direction as we put beliefs and goals into practice. Purpose lets us teach with intention where practices "flow" from beliefs as "we do what we do *with purpose*, with good reason" (Miller 2008, 5).

Excellent teachers insist on saying "no" to some things and "yes" to others. They say "no" to passive activities and "yes" to meaningful literacy. They say "no" to the teacher's desk and "yes" to interacting with their students as they actively engage in real literacy experiences. They say "no" to round-robin reading and "yes" to oral reading with purpose. And they pose critical questions that drive their efforts (Stanier 2008):

Do I say "yes" to the things that matter?

Do I say "no" to the things that don't matter?

Do I have the wisdom to know the difference?

So what do we say "no" to? Linda Hoyt has a valid suggestion as a starting point:

Curricular demands are greater than ever and teachers feel pressured to cover content quickly. I am concerned, however, that the very teachers who have told me there isn't enough time for silent reading are assigning acrostics, fill-in-the-blank sheets, or coloring. If we are to do great work, we must take learning time very seriously and get rid of projects or activities with little credibility. (email message to author, September 21, 2011)

Once we begin saying "no," we can say "yes" to engaging students in authentic, meaningful, and purposeful learning as we invite them to participate in enthusiastic literacy again and again. We can now structure our day "so that books freely chosen and voluminous reading become the 'beating hearts' of our curriculum" (Atwell 2011).

A Little at a Time is a wonderful book about a boy and his grandfather (Adler 2010). After a day filled with questions, he asks his grandfather how he learned so much. His grandfather replies, "I'm just like you. I ask many questions, and little by little I learn a lot. As long as I keep asking, I'll keep learning *a little at a time.*"

Our spotlight teachers are achieving the great work they desire by asking questions in a reflective process. They are not looking for perfection, but to continuously improve the quality of their instruction. Questions help us formulate goals, keeping them in sight as we work toward the action steps that elevate our practices. Each new question moves us one step closer to "serious, thoughtful, informed, responsible, state-of-the-art teaching" (Zemelman, Daniels, and Hyde 2012, 2). This takes personal commitment and dedicated effort to work ever closer to great work—a little at a time.

CHAPTER 3

Sharpening Our Student Lens to Accommodate Targeted Differentiation

> *When we walk into a room where great work is taking place, it's remarkable. The teacher is interacting purposefully, lovingly, and respectfully, providing just-right instruction to nudge students forward. There is a low buzzing hum from students who are comfortable and happy, engaged in their perfectly suited work. It feels like magic, but it isn't. It is great work."*
>
> (Gail Boushey and Joan Moser, email message to author, September 25, 2011)

I have a dirty little secret. There—I said it, garnering courage as we've bonded. What's my elephant in the closet? In 1992, I was given a remarkable gift wrapped neatly in a Reading Recovery® special delivery. I recall each instant of this deeply rewarding learning opportunity. In one awe-inspiring year, I amassed knowledge that continues to reside in each beat of my professional heart.

My dirty little secret is the years prior to my training since I was now painfully aware how much I still had to learn. I saw good work interspersed with newly recognized bad work, but the level of great work I desperately desired and felt I'd achieved suddenly faded from view. I sadly thought about all of the children I had unwittingly slighted in my cognitively lean, pre–Marie Clay years.

Three lessons rose from this life-changing experience. First, I realized great work connects research *and* practice as new understandings alter our perspective. Second, I saw great work as a tentative process of trial and error—as hesitant early steps—and this bolstered my confidence to break free. Finally, I saw students as informative guides I could trust to point me in the right direction. They were my lesson plans waiting to be written as long as I could notice the signposts along the way and respond accordingly.

Steele refers to this as *inspired responses*, as students "show us how to teach them if we remain open to the clues they send" (2010/2011, 67). Excellent teachers can "see possibilities where others see interruptions" (68). They acknowledge that listening, watching, and noticing unexpected opportunities illuminate teachable moments that are invisible when we simply follow a teaching script. You just can't script great work.

Instructional freedom makes us accountable because it forces us to abandon less effective options for those that warrant our time and energy. When Einstein was asked what he needed at Princeton in 1935, he requested a desk, pads, pencils, and a large wastebasket *to hold his mistakes*. We too must be willing to discard potential missteps for the sake of our students. Excellent teachers make these choices every day.

In this chapter, we'll learn how to sharpen our student lens to ensure targeted differentiation. We'll learn to notice signals to address student needs when they arise. We'll learn to reduce whole-group activities and increase small-group and one-to-one learning to maximize our learning time. We'll learn to substitute bad work for good work and accept that good work may not be good enough. "Good is the enemy of great. And that is one of the key reasons why we have so little that becomes great" (Collins 2001, 1).

To demonstrate, let's visit Sarah Bruehl's first-grade classroom in Lawton, Oklahoma. Sarah was one of two first-grade teachers selected for Reading Recovery training during the two years I worked with her. She had become concerned that something was missing in her teaching, so she set out to alter her instructional landscape. After much personal reflection, goal setting, and discussion, she realized that the missing ingredient was targeted differentiation. Let's visit Sarah's classroom at the end of our work together as she puts targeted differentiation into action.

 SPOTLIGHT TEACHER

Putting Great Work into Practice:
Sarah Bruehl, Grade 1: Targeted Differentiation

From the moment I enter Sarah's classroom, I feel positive energy that never wavers. Sarah devotes two hours to eight fifteen-minute rotations. She begins in a whole-class setting as students gather around an easel for a writing workshop lesson. This first session combines teacher modeling and shared practice as they record a message on a chart as teachable moments rise naturally from the print to support her instructional goals. Students then disperse for their first independent rotation as Sarah gathers three students at a table for an interactive writing activity. After generating a message, she supports trial-and-error exploration of sounds and words at the top of an open page. Each word is added in a sentence at the bottom as Sarah encourages the students to use what they know with support as needed. After fifteen minutes, students move to the second whole-class session. She has carefully selected a book for a shared reading to support her goals. They read together, joining enthusiastically in a choral reading while stopping occasionally to frame a word in the book or record it on the chart. Students move to a second rotation as Sarah calls three more students. A third whole-class session focuses on word work that incorporates her goals and observations from earlier rotations. Today students generate words to fit a pattern from the book. They move to a new rotation as she calls one more group. They gather for a final whole-class session of interactive read-aloud

FIGURE 3.1 **Sarah can provide more individualized support in a very small-group setting**

with a lively text about bugs. The morning ends with a final independent rotation with options. Most select a favorite "writing laptop" activity, turning a notebook sideways to write a personal message like the teacher-supported journal. Sarah rotates around the room to interact individually with students. They are constantly engaged in independent, partner, or teacher-supported experiences and a low hum fills the air as a barely audible signal that learning is the order of the day.

While this is impressive under any circumstances, it's even more impressive that it occurred one week before the end of the year and just after learning the school was clos-ing. It was an emotionally draining time and all instructional material was packed in preparation for the final days, but Sarah didn't allow this "glitch" to interfere with her responsibility to students. She simply faced this challenging time head on with shorter rotation blocks. No excuses, complaints, or unwelcome activities intruded on her day because Sarah is committed to going about the business of learning in spite of distrac-tions that are part of our world—as any excellent teacher would do.

Sarah's transformation was due in part to professional development opportunities. But this alone was not enough to transform her practices. Sarah had to recognize the inadequacy of her literacy program to meet students' needs and make adjustments that would elevate her teaching. Her tipping point (Gladwell 2002) was to notice and discard bad work so she could make room for more good work and newfound great work.

- dedicated block of time devoted exclusively to literacy (two hours)
- independent literacy activities supported by extensive modeling and practice
- student independence explicitly taught and reinforced on a regular basis
- differentiated instruction viewed as a non-negotiable part of the learning day
- targeted instruction through small groups or one-to-one experiences

OVERVIEW OF SARAH'S TWO-HOUR LITERACY BLOCK			
Time	Minutes	Setting	Activity Focus
9:30–9:45	15	whole class	Writing workshop (I Do/We Do)
9:45–10:00	15	small group	Independent rotation/small group (You Do)
10:00–10:15	15	whole class	Shared reading (I Do/We Do)
10:15–10:30	15	small group	Independent rotation/small group (You Do)
10:30–10:45	15	whole class	Word work (I Do/We Do)
10:45–11:00	15	small group	Independent rotation/small group (You Do)
11:00–11:15	15	whole class	Interactive read-aloud (I Do/We Do)
11:15–11:30	15	one-to-one	Independent rotation/small group (You Do)

- consistently very small groups of three to four students
- whole-class lessons designed to build on and support learning goals
- informational texts viewed as central to a total literacy experience

I had the pleasure to support and witness Sarah's changes, but any teacher can accomplish the same transformation with a commitment to reflective teaching. Sarah continues to alter her literacy program with students as the inspiration. During our last session, I asked Sarah to reflect on how her teaching has changed.

SARAH'S INSTRUCTIONAL TRANSFORMATION OVER TIME	
Then	Now
• all recommended worksheets	• selective use of worksheets
• limited student independence	• explicitly teach for independence
• mainly whole-group instruction	• mainly one-to-one and small group
• isolated skill-and-drill	• authentic application of skills
• trivial seatwork activities	• meaningful seatwork activities
• sporadic engagement in literacy	• active engagement in literacy
• limited view of reading	• balanced view of reading
• passive learning experiences	• hands-on learning experiences
• disorganized literacy structure	• highly organized literacy structure
• heavy reliance on teachers' guides	• emphasis on professional judgment
• focus on grade-level instruction	• focus on differentiated instruction

Sarah's transformation illustrates two critical features of instructional change. First, she intentionally scaffolds her teaching to reinforce and promote strategies so students can work independently. Second, she acknowledges the value of flexible groupings that focus on targeted support. Whole-group instruction prevented her from meeting student needs. She began to see that targeted differentiation, or small-group and individual support, was the missing ingredient so she adjusted her day accordingly. Sarah established a goal and refused to let anything stand in the way of achieving that goal.

Personal Investigation of Instructional Grouping Activities

Flexible grouping is a central component of targeted differentiation, so let's begin this chapter by analyzing our grouping practices. Allington suggests accomplishing this by tallying whole-group, small-group, and side-by-side experiences at a schoolwide level (2009, 40). We'll use our next form to adapt his suggestion using a personal professional tool to support our move toward more targeted differentiation.

The form gives us a visual breakdown of grouping activities in a reading block for one week. This visual reference is a concrete way to uncover areas of need that may be hidden without closer inspection. Each square is ten minutes (a half slash is five minutes) to give you a written record of how much time you spend in each category. At the end of the week, add the total minutes and divide that sum by the minutes in the weekly reading block. Now multiply by one hundred for a breakdown of your grouping.

The sample reflects that Lesley, our spotlight teacher from Chapter 1, knows that a large percentage of her reading block time is needed for small groups and one-to-one opportunities. The pie chart shows her the distribution of her day at a glance and reflects where she may need to make adjustments. Over time, a visual picture of her teaching will emerge. While she will need to spend more time in whole-group activities initially as she promotes stamina and independence, the form helps her keep this focus in view.

The form mirrors your instructional priorities and is a helpful tool as you work to incorporate targeted options. As you look at your breakdown, notice if you offer a range of differentiated support. This makes it easy to ensure that all students receive support in some form, although your most struggling readers will need more frequent and intensive support opportunities. Continue using the form until smaller groupings become part of your instructional repertoire. Great work is impossible without more targeted support, so make this your priority.

FIGURE 3.2 **Lesley visually views her teaching as she makes small incremental changes for her fifth graders**

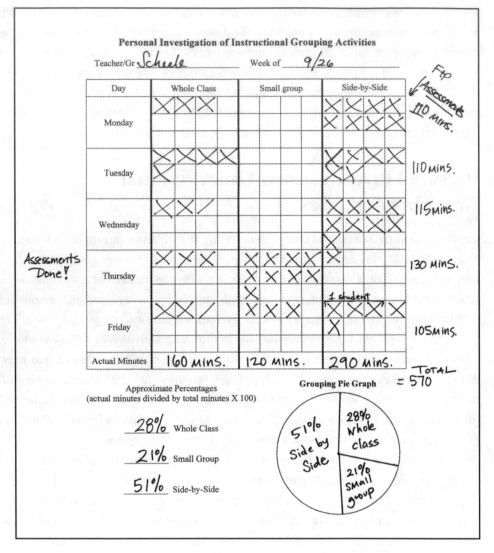

Using an Instructional Menu of Options to Sharpen Our Student Lens

A common characteristic of the teachers described in this book is their willingness to use varied instructional contexts. This critical feature of differentiation, knowing how and when to use these instructional groupings, helps us meet the needs of all students. A menu of instructional options, chosen with care, allows us to accommodate a wide range of learners. The visual in Figure 3.3 shows the variety of options that must be in place.

These varied options broaden the range of learning opportunities so we aren't constrained by grade-level expectations that ignore reading needs. While we include whole-class teacher-supported activities, it is only one aspect of a menu of possibilities. We also acknowledge that smaller settings for targeted support are needed, particularly for those below grade level. This isn't an either-or proposition since each has a distinct purpose. We sharpen a blurry lens by broadening our scope so our students can achieve success no matter where they fall in the learning spectrum.

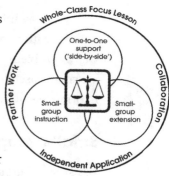

FIGURE 3.3 **Instructional Options in a Differentiated Classroom**

A brief description follows of the instructional options we use to accommodate student needs. In Chapter 4, we will explore how to mix and match these options as we prioritize our instructional goals.

Whole-Class Focus Lessons

Whole-class activities reflect the outer circle of our range of options where we embrace all learners using common goals and experiences to set the stage for targeted support. These minilessons can be ten- to thirty-minute sessions that address specific instructional points. They generally occur in teacher-supported contexts such as read-aloud or shared reading. We can use more complex texts since flexible support ensures success.

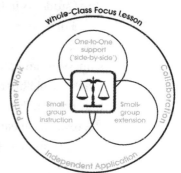

Our focus lesson is then an instructional springboard into flexible small-group learning reflected in the bottom circles. Our selection depends on our instructional purpose and whether we can ensure that each member of the group will be equally engaged, accountable, and successful throughout the learning activity (Marzano, Pickering, and Pollock 2004).

Small-Group Instruction (Homogeneous)

We may form small groups with a single text and common focus that can arise from the whole-class learning experience or be distinctive to those students' learning needs. These groups are flexible and dynamic so we don't assign group names that result in static groupings that rarely change. Groups are formed using both reading level and reading behaviors to address a common need or learning goal. These groups change as students grow.

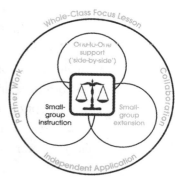

We may initiate small-group instruction if we have a learning goal we want to address with a carefully matched text. These high-success texts build independence as well as problem-solving behaviors that develop as students work out tricky parts. Groups are small based on student need, ranging from three to five students, and generally occur in brief sessions lasting fifteen to twenty minutes.

Small-Group Extension (Heterogeneous)

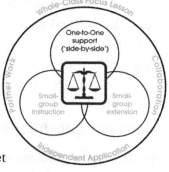

Unlike small-group instruction, these heterogeneous small-group extensions focus on self-selected independent texts. We may still have a common goal, but independent texts make it easy to accommodate wide reading ranges. These are smaller groups of shorter duration, generally two or three students in five- to seven-minute sessions.

For example, we may bring three students together to discuss characters, the author's purpose, reading with expression, summarization, or text choice. We may ask students to find a sample that will illustrate a point or share a favorite part based on the discussion focus. They may read orally to support the goal, but this occurs with meaning and expression because the texts are at each child's independent reading level. These high-interest, self-selected texts also increase motivation.

One-to-One Targeted Support

We also need opportunities for one-to-one (or side-by-side) learning. These brief informal activities are generally just two to five minutes, but these are powerful minutes. We again use student-selected independent texts to create both an emotionally and academically rewarding interaction with the teacher. This setting makes it easy to adjust learning goals and the limited time allows us to meet with all students at least weekly.

Both texts and readers vary widely, giving us unlimited opportunities within this grouping option. We may listen to a child read or initiate a conference, use a text to help the child read at a slower pace, or promote reading with meaning. This is a good time to collect an informal assessment such as a reading record or to assess comprehension.

Partner Work and Peer Collaboration

Peer collaboration allows us to relinquish responsibility to students while freeing us to interact with students in smaller settings. We may rotate to support students' efforts, engage in kidwatching (Goodman 1978), or initiate teacher-supported learning. Peer engagement allows students to independently apply learning in supportive contexts.

This wide range of rich instructional options for peer work is an excellent time to achieve more great work. We may work with a group to support their efforts, conduct a small-group guided reading activity, or work with a student individually. This is a good time to gather anecdotal notes as we rotate among students to observe them as they work together. These recorded observations are helpful in planning new learning opportunities.

Independent Application

Independence is the ultimate goal of teaching, so we want to be sure that we offer time for students to work unsupported so they can apply learning at easy or independent levels. We are careful not to push students to independence too quickly, so they will have the tools that will help them to achieve a high degree of success.

Again, this is a good time to confer with individual students or to rotate around the room to observe students as they work on their own. We can gather additional informal assessment information by asking questions, taking a reading record, or engaging students in conversations that revolve around learning. This may lead to any of the instructional options described as our growing knowledge helps us make new choices.

Making the Most of Your Instructional Groupings

Some teachers spend the bulk of their day in a small-group setting where more intensive support is needed. Debbie is a Title 1 teacher in Sunapee, New Hampshire, with sixteen years of experience in kindergarten through grade 2. In this lesson, Debbie is learning to sharpen her student lens with two first-grade boys.

SPOTLIGHT
TEACHER

Debbie Shapiro, Title 1: Initial Teaching Activity

Two boys enthusiastically sit at the table with a book in their hands. Debbie begins by drawing attention to the word *around*. She adds this word to their word file and asks them to read the word several times. She tells them she highlighted the word in the book with orange tape to look for as they read. She asks them what strategies they can use if they come to a tricky word. They discuss several options and she reminds them to use those strategies as they read. The students read brief sections softly at their own pace as Debbie listens individually. She draws attention to any strategy they use ("I noticed . . . ") or prompts them if they get stuck ("What can you try?"). The students begin to wait until she turns her attention to their reading. After each page, she reinforces strategies she notices and engages students in lively discussion revolving around the content. She continuously refers to her observations to reinforce learning. After reading, she tells them to select any animal and write three animal clues for their partner to guess. She thinks aloud, adding clues to the board so they can guess her animal. She gives them a dry erase board to do this on their own. They write clues enthusiastically and guess the animals. As they leave, it is apparent they have enjoyed this engaging activity.

Debriefing Session

We began by discussing the many successful components of Debbie's lesson:

- very small group for focused support
- high-interest texts carefully matched to students
- high-frequency word building (*around*)
- emphasis on strategy use in context
- teacher modeling and think-aloud
- faded support with shared and independent application
- reading and writing as a reciprocal process

Debbie demonstrates a deep understanding of her students and the reading process that is central to great work. Meaningful talk is expertly woven into the lesson to support and extend understanding as she moves from known to new. Her lesson reflects good work, but Debbie wants to achieve great work. The following bullets capture our conversation to accomplish her desired move from good to great.

- **Let the word rise from the experience.** Students should take responsibility by writing words on a card or dry erase board or by highlighting or framing the word in the text.

- **Set a clear purpose for reading.** Write the purpose on a sentence strip and keep it in full view. This will make the purpose more concrete while making it easy to revisit that purpose often.

- **Create a strategy tool.** Initiate strategy bookmarks to provide a concrete reference in the context of reading. In this way, strategies are seen integral to, not separate from, the act of reading.

- **Use an activity that rises from the text.** Take advantage of examples in the text. Having students be the "expert" of one page will reinforce the initial selection with a meaningful repeated reading experience.

Follow-Up Teaching Sequence (with My Reflection in Parentheses)

Debbie uses the same book since they didn't finish it in the last session (depth over breadth). She revisits a page and asks them to frame a word with their index fingers and then highlight the word with the tape (student responsibility). Debbie displays a sentence strip and asks them to find the word (frequent review). She uses this to set her purpose (recorded sense of direction). She reads a page they read earlier and thinks aloud as she generates clues from the book to write on the board (teacher model). Students are then assigned an "expert" page (student as expert). She tells them their job is to read the page and write clues from the book to help their partner guess the animal (text-based focus). As they work on their own, she listens to them read or talks about their clues as both boys are constantly engaged (time on task). As they use a strategy, this is written on a strategy bookmark they can add to later (concrete strategy tool).

FIGURE 3.4 **Debbie sets a clear purpose in writing for a more focused learning activity**

My strategy bookmark

Think!

look for clues

Read again

Find a chunk

use the pictures

Talk about it

they

make connections

Find new books

FIGURE 3.5 **Student-Created Strategy Bookmark**

Debbie knows that very small groups afford her students intensive support in a positive environment. She knows each minute counts and ensures success by promoting independence and offering support at just-right moments. She values time on task and makes sure reading, writing, and talking are her primary goals. But it is Debbie's desire and determination to achieve more great work that is moving her closer to that lofty goal.

To support Debbie's strategy focus, students can personalize a strategy bookmark during reading. This is not just a list of strategies (What *would* you do?) but opportunities to explore them in context (What *did* you do?). This also gives students a personalized reference tool that will grow with them to reinforce and support strategies as they arise.

Teachers like Debbie spend their days exclusively in small-group settings, but we can use a mix-and-match approach to satisfy a wide variety of purposes. A flexible view allows us to initiate learning in a whole-class setting, promote that goal in more intensive settings, and then culminate the learning activity by returning to a whole-class setting.

Let's return to Lesley Scheele's fifth-grade classroom to see this mix-and-match view in action. When we first met Lesley in Chapter 1, she was learning to integrate whole-class and small-group instruction. She introduced a class anchor chart in a whole-class activity and then in small groups. Lesley's personal goal was to broaden this range of flexible options by more effectively blending whole-class, small-group, and one-to-one learning. She has since exceeded this goal through coordinated flexible instruction.

FIGURE 3.6 **A personal bookmark reinforces strategy use in the context of the reading activity**

Lesley Scheele, Grade 5:
Integrating Varied Instructional Options

Lesley understands that explicitly teaching and supporting metacognitive strategies is a critical goal. She is helping students make text connections using schema, but she has become increasingly concerned they are making connections thoughtlessly as if checking off their "to-do" list. She wants them to understand how to connect their thinking to texts at deeper levels, but she knows this requires repeated opportunities and explicit models.

To support a move to deeper levels of comprehension, Lesley created a class anchor chart: "Connection! So What?" She introduced the chart in a whole-class setting to model her own thinking first. Now she can pause during reading to share her ideas (*Connection!*) and think aloud about how it helps her as a reader (*So What?*) as students record their connections in a "Thinker's Notebook." She emphasizes good readers use schema, or prior knowledge, to make connections, but they also understand how schema helps them to deepen their thinking as readers.

After the whole-class session, Lesley reinforces this strategy in small-group, one-to-one, and partner work—as well as independent experiences. The chart is the focal point of learning in each setting and provides a long-term reference tool students can revisit and add to in this and other learning activities. This cross-text learning over time is important for the deeper understanding she wants to achieve. It also reframes small groups as another opportunity to accomplish the same learning goals so that whole-class and small-group activities have a common instructional purpose.

FIGURE 3.7 **Lesley introduces a common learning goal with an anchor chart as students reflect in their thinker's notebook**

FIGURE 3.8 **The class anchor chart now becomes a focal point for teacher-supported instruction**

Web form 5

Varied Instructional Grouping Activity Planning Form

Topic/ Focus _Activating Schema_   Date 9/26/ – 9/30

Small Group Activity Description	**One-to-One Support**

Small Group Activity Description

☑ Instruction (homogeneous) ☐ Extension (heterogeneous)
- In small groups this week we will use the same anchor chart (w/ new stickies) to plot connections + deeper understanding while we read.
- We will read an article from Nat. Geo. Magazine (on Ocean Life)
- There will be plenty of stickies for kids to use + write conn. + understandings
- Kids will hang up stickies as the write them + together they will create 1 chart.

Whole Class Description

☑ BEFORE small groups   ☐ AFTER small groups
→ Introduce Connection So what? Chart/ form as an anchor chart
→ Explain making connections is imp. BUT only if it improves comprehension.
→ Read _What You Know First_ aloud to kids (prob 1/2 the book 1st day)
→ Think aloud + fill the chart w/ Connections + "So whats"
→ After a few pgs. open it up to the whole class too
→ Add to the chart as kids share

One-to-One Support

When I confer 1:1 w/ kids this week I will encourage them to "track" connections + "so whats" in their Thinker's Notebooks. My hope is that this 1:1 attention will help bridge the success in whole/small gr. and help all kids become more strategic/ deeper thinkers. Pay particular attention to:
· Andre
· Logan
· Caylin
· Corbyn

On Your Own   1. Peer Collaboration   2. Independent Application
1. When pair or Buddy Reading kids will tune into each others connections + politely ask: "So what".
2. When Ind. Reading kids will start tracking using connection forms.

FIGURE 3.9 **Lesley reflects on her instructional goals to make adjustments that will enhance her teaching**

FIGURE 3.10 **Class Anchor Chart on Making Connections**

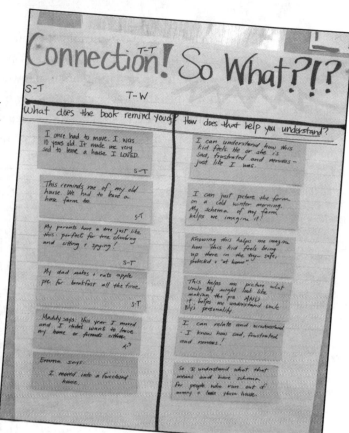

Lesley's goal to reach across multiple instructional settings requires her concentrated effort to continuously fine-tune her own learning. She is beginning to move seamlessly between whole-class modeling, shared and guided practice, partner work, and independent application. Her students are actively engaged in each setting, applying learning in high-success texts at varying levels of support, and she is using concrete references of learning to promote new learning in varied instructional experiences.

Lesley knows that putting her thinking in writing makes it more concrete and helps her notice if students need support. She uses our second planning and reflection form of the chapter as a tool. She records her plan in writing and is continuously aware whether students are successful or whether she needs to consider new directions.

After the lesson, Lesley reflected on her success through her students' eyes: "I was amazed that by the end of the week, all of my kids (even the most tangled learners) understood what to do and were beginning to do it independently."

Lesley's determination to achieve excellence in and across instructional settings has changed her as a teacher because these flexible options have now become ingrained into her instructional repertoire. Her goal has been achieved through dedicated daily practice. Through this dedicated effort, flexible grouping options are now part of who Lesley is and what she believes as a teacher.

To ensure Lesley offers the instructional support students need, she uses our final form in this chapter (see Figure 3.11). So we don't leave to chance whether we successfully meet the needs of our students, we can keep a written reference to track those opportunities. A visual reference of the week ensures that Lesley offers varied instructional support and allows her to quickly determine if she is addressing the learning needs of every student.

Lesley lists student names on the left and notes support options used in the columns. She can quickly see her individual and small-group supports. She color-codes students she wants to pay attention to that week with pink for daily support, yellow for three to four times that week, and blue for two or three times that week. The star on the right emphasizes students she knows will need continued support next week. This makes it easy to set aside the time warranted so that no child falls through the cracks.

FIGURE 3.11 **A visual reference of our teaching makes it easy to see where more support may be needed**

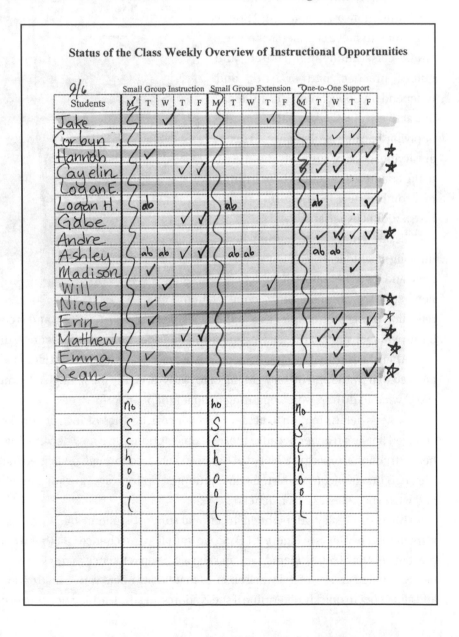

Status of the Class Weekly Overview of Instructional Opportunities

Lesley knows that teaching to the middle according to a grade-level designation is professionally irresponsible considering the varied needs of her class. A menu of options gives her alternatives for a personalized approach to differentiation. If "whole class" is the only instructional option, our lens is blurred for students above or below grade level. She can now offer targeted support and still meet the needs of more proficient learners.

Adjusting Our Instructional Perspective from "Struggling" to "Capable" Learners

Sarah, Debbie, and Lesley have demonstrated how to sharpen our instructional lens. Our students make the quality of our work transparent and targeted differentiation is our moral obligation to *our* students. We can't depend on others to do this because thirty minutes of success won't make up for five hours of frustration. Students need "a full classroom reading lesson offered at their level every day, and it is the classroom teacher who must provide this" (Allington 2010, 2).

The quality of instruction is particularly critical for struggling readers. Clay suggests students identified as learning disabled may in fact be *instructionally disabled* due to a mismatch in the instruction they get and the instruction they need (1987). We exacerbate the problem with instructionally ineffective solutions that sidetrack us from the high-quality instruction that comes only from knowledgeable teachers (Allington 2012b).

Our discussions about high-quality literacy must also take a closer look at what happens the entire school day. Regardless of other supports in place, we pay particular attention to the quality of the general education classroom. If more than 20 percent of students in general education are not successful, then we may need to take a closer look at the quality of that instruction (Dorn and Soffos 2012; Dorn and Schubert 2008).

This is complicated by overemphasis on scripted programs that may lead to a false sense of security. Scripted programs can't address the instructional complexity and range of needs and fail to build professional expertise, leading to a "teaching disability" (Applegate, Applegate, and Turner 2010). Worse, they are rarely put through the rigors of research suggested (Dewitz, Leahy, Jones, and Sullivan 2010). Yet billions of dollars are wasted on these one-size-fits-all core programs "that seem to offer an easy solution for plummeting literacy levels" (Cooter and Perkins 2011, 563).

"Fidelity contracts" are another frightening new practice—using contractual promises to "faithfully follow the often-scripted programs that sometimes conflict with their [teachers'] visions of best practice" (Turner, Applegate, and Applegate 2011, 551). Fidelity contracts may need a warning label: "Great work of knowledgeable professionals is hereby forbidden." A new term, "kid-delity," may refocus our responsibility where it belongs—on our students.

The truth is that *all* students need expert teachers who insist on active engagement in meaningful reading, reciprocity of reading and writing, skills in context, and emphasis on strategic knowledge. Yet *flexible* approaches such as Reading Recovery (Clay 1985), Comprehensive Intervention Model (Dorn and Schubert 2008; Dorn and Soffos 2012), or Interactive Strategies Approach (Scanlon and Anderson 2010) are rare—and Leveled Literacy Intervention (Fountas and Pinnell 2008a, 2008b, 2008c) is unique in that it acknowledges professional judgment. Why?

Teacher expertise is not a minor point since it grants us the common sense we need to recognize questionable ideas or use alternate routes to avoid them. We can't ignore that great work requires expert, knowledgeable teachers, particularly for struggling readers. "An average amount of basic reading knowledge might suffice for many children, but for children who struggle, more expertise is needed" (Johnson 2006, 3).

We must also guard against labels with a "deficit" lens (what students *can't* do) over a "generative" lens (what students *can* do) (Enriquez, Jones, and Clarke 2010, 73). Vygotsky referred to this as "positive differentiation" (Gindis 1999). "If we continue to believe that some students can just be expected to be struggling readers, then there will be little reason to work to ensure all students become literate" (Allington 2010, 5).

Good teachers "constantly search for effective ways to serve the children they teach" (Pinnell and Fountas 2009, 3). They don't label students as "struggling" but explore what they can do to alter that course. "When students achieve as readers, many other facets of effective teaching and learning come into high relief. The children's reading advances, they are thinking, happier, more engaged, and on task" (Taylor 2011, 1).

Addressing Key Motivation Factors to Elevate and Support Our Instructional Efforts

In order to offer our support options, first we must address the three motivation factors at the center of our visual: resources, organization, and environment. They set the stage for differentiation and free our time for individualized support.

These factors are central to great work, yet these are often missing ingredients in practice and were notably ignored in the National Reading Panel Report (National Institute of Child Health and Human Development 2000). As a result, there has been near hyperfocus on the "five pillars": phonemic awareness, phonics, fluency, vocabulary, and comprehension. Oddly, motivation didn't even warrant a quick nod.

While it's hard to argue their relevance, or their interrelationship and relative value, how much or how long attention is warranted on the five pillars, or other equally relevant factors, *is* debatable. Comprehensive literacy (Pressley 2007) must include "motivation; opportunities to read and write; differentiated assessment and instruction; and reading, writing, listening, and speaking for wide, authentic and varied purposes" (Gambrell, Malloy, and Mazzoni 2011).

Motivation is central to great work since high-success daily reading can increase skills in almost every area (Krashen 2004, 2011). We want our students to view reading from Miller's viewpoint: "I am a reader, a flashlight-under-the-covers, carries-a-book-everywhere-I-go, don't-look-at-my-Amazon-bill reader" (2009, 11).

FIGURE 3.12 **Key Motivation Factors**

The motivation factors of organization, environment, and resources are addressed only briefly here, since our spotlight teachers highlight these in greater detail.

Organization: An organizational structure makes the flexible menu of literacy options feasible. We must consider everything including scheduling, grouping, and room design so we can quickly put our varied options in place.

Environment: A learning environment reflects "incredible insight into its culture and the teachers' understanding of literacy practices" (Campbell Hill and Ekey 2010). Classroom environments beckon readers and writers to participate in joyful literacy.

Resources: We can't promote literacy with a "dearth of interesting material" (Gallagher 2009). High-quality resources include a well-stocked classroom library of inviting texts. Independent texts and ample opportunities to enjoy them is the heart and soul of great work.

FIGURE 3.13 **These first-grade readers remind us to engage students in meaningful, enthusiastic literacy from the earliest grades**

As we address these critical motivation factors, we keep these things in mind:

- clear areas designated for whole-class and small-group learning

- wide variety of high-quality texts for whole-class, teacher-supported activities

- organized independent library arranged by categories such as topic, genre, or author

- tubs filled with books that revolve around a topic or theme at varied levels

- book boxes or book bags for students to store their personal selections

- clipboards to bring students close or to "take learning on the move"

- sticky notes to create learning references that make learning public

- learning displays and references to support and extend ongoing goals

- wall spaces that celebrate daily learning and grow with students

- heavy emphasis on high-success engaging literacy experiences

FIGURE 3.14 **A rich learning environment invites daily literacy engagement**

Motivation, with key factors of organization, environment, and resources, is the glue of an effective literacy classroom. Through these factors, daily engagement in whole-class, small-group, one-to-one, or collaborative learning in or across grades will become the very foundation of our teaching. Maybe Hollimon's simple view is right: read more, write more, and teach vocabulary (2011). Without active literacy at the center, great work is forever out of our reach.

Creating a Classroom Culture That Places Active Literacy Engagement at the Center

Two characteristics exemplify our spotlight teachers. First, they create full days of reading, writing, and talking where substance is valued over "stuff." Second, they believe that success is the right of every learner and guarantee that right as they acknowledge and celebrate whatever their students may bring to the literacy table.

We need to be sure we place our energy and focus our discussions on the very issues defined by these characteristics. A good starting point is to establish schoolwide standards to increase the volume of reading (Allington 2012a). Any teacher who fails to

FIGURE 3.15 **Cross-grade literacy opportunities broaden our ability to support literacy**

acknowledge the goal of voluminous reading will never experience the sheer delight of enthusiastic learning in classrooms where every child soars to success. And that would be a tragic loss for all involved.

In the end, we are responsible if students "never catch up with their higher-achieving classmates because schools create school days for them where they struggle all day long" (Allington 2009, 1). The truth is that these students have much to teach us about great work as expressed by Hoyt, Davis, Olson, and Boswell:

> *It is our belief that striving readers are an asset—an opportunity to bring out the best in ourselves and our practice—and that the diversity of need that they bring to our classrooms gives us the opportunity to do our very best work. (2011, 1–2)*

Our very best work, indeed! Tomlinson and McTighe remind us that "the goal is not perfection but persistence in the pursuit of understanding things" (2006, 56). Each of the teachers described in this book insist on relentless persistent pursuits. They know that grand understandings can occur when they are face-to-face in the most intimate of settings. They know they can learn much about literacy and its many challenges in these settings through their students' eyes. Most of all, they know that our students are our best teachers if we keep our hearts and minds open to the lessons they have in store for us. And *that* is great work at its finest!

CHAPTER 4

Designing an Inclusive Instructional Plan that Allows Time for More Great Work

> ❝ *I've been privileged to observe highly effective teachers in action. They differ in many respects, but their great work nearly always rests on a single trait; they are resolutely focused. They teach less content in much greater depth over a long period of time and provide myriad ways for children to apply what they learn. Our children deserve that focus; in fact their learning depends on it.*❞
>
> (ELLIN KEENE, EMAIL MESSAGE TO AUTHOR, SEPTEMBER 27, 2011)

I too have had the privilege to observe highly effective teachers in action. I see teachers fine-tune instructional practices to maximize time with students. I see teachers challenge themselves in ways that make students the rich benefactors of their dedicated efforts. I see teachers acknowledge excellence as a never-ending process of professional learning. I see teachers willingly make adjustments that will increase the quality of their teaching. And I see both inexperienced and veteran teachers who are resolutely focused on a singular goal—doing more great work in the name of their students.

In Chapter 3, we explored a menu of grouping options to sharpen our student lens with whole-class, small-group, one-to-one, peer-supported, and independent learning. In this chapter, we look at the central features of high-quality literacy instruction and see teachers making these flexible learning opportunities a priority. These fluid experiences promote a broader view of differentiation based on professional decision making.

Let's begin with thirty-year veteran third-grade teacher Betsy Glad from Cedar Ridge Elementary in Tulsa, Oklahoma. Betsy will demonstrate how expert teachers create inclusive learning opportunities that reflect the critical attributes of differentiation. As you read, notice how Betsy intentionally weaves language that entices and instructs. Betsy's exact words are in bold type so you can experience learning from her eyes.

FIGURE 4.1 **Betsy uses an anchor chart to record inner conversations during reading**

FIGURE 4.2 **Betsy gradually relinquishes responsibility to students as they apply learning**

Putting Great Work into Practice:
Betsy Glad, Grade 3: Whole-Class Read-Aloud with Varied Support Options

Betsy calls students to the gathering area where she gently cradles a book on her lap. She shows them the cover as some heads nod in recognition. **I'm excited some of you will experience this book again and others will experience it for the first time. If you read it before, see if you notice anything new.** They nod as if to accept her challenge. *The Wall* (1992) is a book by Eve Bunting about a father and his young son who go to the Vietnam Memorial Wall to find the name of the grandfather the little boy never knew. She pauses so they can take a closer look at the cover. **You can see the father and his son looking at names on the wall. They look so sad. I never met my grandfather, so I made a connection because I know how the little boy must feel. We make connections when we use our experiences to understand and enjoy reading. Turn and talk to your elbow partner about a connection you make as you look at the cover.** They talk briefly. **We've discussed how good readers use expression to make reading flow like butter. That helps us with comprehension so I'll do that as I read. We've been talking about comprehension. What does that mean?** A child responds, "Am I understanding what I'm reading?" **Thank you for sharing that secret about reading. Nothing is more important than our thinking when we read.** She opens the book to the first page. **As I read, I'll use my inner voice to have a conversation in my head. My inner voice helps me go to a deeper level of understanding as a reader.** She holds up sticky notes. **I'm going to write down my ideas because active readers leave tracks of their thinking just like animals leave tracks in the snow. I'll jot down quick notes about ideas and questions that really matter to me so I can hold and remember my thoughts.** She reads the first page and stops. **I had an inner conversation and**

FIGURE 4.3 **Sticky notes provide a concrete tool to leave tracks on their thinking**

I want to jot that down so I won't forget. She writes on a sticky note. Now I know that the grandfather was killed in a war so I understand why they're so sad. She puts the sticky note on the page. As she reads, she pauses to share her inner conversations as she thinks aloud. I wonder why the boy calls it his grandfather's wall? I had a lightbulb moment when I saw the soldier in a wheelchair. I think maybe he was injured in the war. I think the date 1969 is important so I'll write it down so I can remember. I used my schema because I know about the Memorial Wall. I'll read this part again to slow down my thinking. Students are mesmerized. She pauses so they can turn and talk as she slowly rotates. I heard amazing ideas. She asks for volunteers to share their inner conversations. A child shares that his grandfather was in the war while another child likes the way they covered the names with paper so they can see them. You saw me make tracks in my thinking and now you'll do that too. She distributes clipboards with three sticky notes. Quality is important, so I'd rather see one good connection that shows you're having an inner conversation than three that don't show you're thinking about your ideas. Leave your own tracks of your thinking as you make connections to the ideas in the book. She moves around the room as students write. Now we'll take our thinking even deeper by sharing. Remember to be a respectful listener. She rotates as they discuss their ideas. She stops and writes on a tablet: "Big Ideas and Lingering Questions." What does *lingering* mean? She compliments a child's explanation that *lingering* is when an idea sticks in your head and adds that these are questions we may want to answer. I think a big idea is that the memorial helps us remember people we lost so I'll write that. They add more examples: Soldiers protect us. Why do people leave things by the wall? When they finish, she briefly reviews. Today we shared inner conversations good readers have as they make connections to their own experiences. When we share our inner conversations, we learn and understand more. We'll keep practicing having inner conversations.

Highlighting Key Instructional Features of Betsy's Read-Aloud Lesson

Betsy's great work is based on extensive personal study and daily reflection on her teaching. Her expertise is the result of dedicated effort, but these qualities are within the reach of any teacher willing to make a commitment to high-quality literacy:

- deep appreciation for literacy by actions and words (*excited, amazing*)
- fluency defined as more than speed (*flows like butter*)

- varied viewpoints acknowledged (*see if you notice anything new*)
- thoughtful language (*connections, schema, inner voice, tracks in thinking*)
- reading/writing connection (*sticky notes, reflection anchor chart*)
- vocabulary connections in a meaningful context (*lingering*)
- think-aloud to illustrate strategies (*I'll read again, slow down my thinking*)
- gradual release of responsibility (*independent and partner work*)
- view of learning as more than a one-shot proposition (*multiple exposure*)

Instructional Partnership:
Jan Gross, Media Specialist

As I arrived, Betsy warned me students would be excited when they returned from the library, where "books are like candy." Jan Gross, media specialist at Betsy's school, nurtures this view. She sees her role as a teacher and instructional partner able to lighten teachers' load by supporting the curriculum. Jan cross-references picture books to show the instructional possibilities at a glance using their professional references (Harvey and Goudvis 2007; Zimmerman and Hutchins 2003; Miller 2002; Keene and Zimmerman 2007; Calkins 2001).

Each labeled bin is filled with picture books to promote strategies in these references. Jan also wrote the genre (biography, historical fiction) and some instructional options (inferencing, self-questioning, visualization, point of view, locating key details) on the front of each book. This helps teachers quickly find a book for a selected strategy focus while individually labeled books illustrate other instructional possibilities. Catego-

FIGURE 4.4 **Jan creates bins of labeled books to give teachers instant access to varied text selections that support specific instructional goals**

rize bins on your own, with a colleague, or through your local library to create curriculum extensions to support your instructional goals. These bins will grow *with* you.

Jan believes "teaching" libraries should say to students, "Come on in as often as you need. Everything here is yours." Therefore, she has a simple book selection guideline: four to five "just-right" books with at least one picture book, one nonfiction, and two for pleasure. We should all echo Jan's heartwarming view of literacy:

- If we give children paperwork, they forget. If we give them beautiful literature where they can make connections, they'll comprehend and retain forever.
- Reading is like a colander where all the good stuff stays at the top and the stuff you don't want or need at the moment just falls through.

- Kids come in different packages. We can't control the package they come with, but they're each entitled to opportunities to become a wonderful reader.

Jan gave me this note as I left: "Reading isn't just behavioral objectives and predictable outcomes. Reading is enjoying, learning, becoming, laughing, crying, sympathizing, and listening to great authors, thus growing into a magnificent reader for life."

Books are viewed like candy when adults who surround students share that view. This is likely mirrored in the homes of more proficient readers, but some students depend on us to promote reading as a pleasurable event. Our actions speak volumes—and our students are listening! I suspect Jan and Betsy would agree with Richard Allington:

> There is no shortage of funding to double the size of classroom and school libraries. But it is now largely wasted on test prep (or software), spelling books, and worksheets that don't have a shred of research support. None! But schools still spend incredible amounts of money purchasing low-level ineffective tools. Imagine the size of classroom libraries if for one year schools gave up unproven materials and invested that money in paperback books! And imagine what would happen to the achievement of poor children if they spent the day engaged in reading and writing instead of low-level materials. In the end, it is professional educators who will decide how funds and school time will be spent. So, next year propose to eliminate these things. Then revel in the reading and writing growth of your students. (email message to author, June 10, 2011)

Determining What Is Essential in Our Teaching to Establish Instructional Priorities

We need guidelines for the mind-set exemplified by Betsy and Jan as the standard we strive to achieve. We use the best research to inform our teaching while understanding what research can and cannot do. Research is "an essential guide to policy and practice" (Duke and Martin 2011, 10), but teacher experience is also critical. Together, expertise and research form the ideal partnership.

This partnership is exemplified in the visual below. We balance text experiences to reinforce and challenge readers while prioritizing independent reading. We offer relevant, meaningful, purposeful, and appropriate opportunities that are motivating, interesting, engaging, and inviting. These features are at the core of great work where literacy forms the invisible thread that weaves through our entire day.

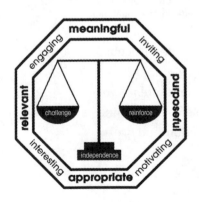

FIGURE 4.5 **Overview of Key Instructional Components**

The Standards for Reading Professionals support our guidelines to ensure "elements of a balanced, integrated, and comprehensive literacy curriculum" (International Reading Association 2010, 9). We also use Petty's 20-80 rule: "Twenty percent of what you do makes 80 percent of the difference, so let's work smarter, not harder, by concentrating on the factors that make the difference" (2009, 3). To help us as we learn to work smarter, we'll highlight seven literacy guidelines.

1. Excellent teachers *see high-quality books as a central learning tool.* Books well chosen elevate our teaching to higher levels of meaning and pleasure. Morrow emphasizes that a literacy program is incomplete without literature (2010). In fact, wide access to books both at school *and* home directly correlates to achievement (Edwards 2011; Neuman and Dickinson 2011; McQuillan 2008).

2. Excellent teachers *view independent reading as a vital literacy component.* They fill the day with teacher- and peer-supported writing and talking to support independent reading. We can't complain about the state of literacy and withhold the one thing that can alter that landscape. Independent reading isn't an "extra" but an "integral part of our balanced literacy program" (Taberski 2011, 31).

3. Excellent teachers *build deeper levels of pleasurable and thoughtful literacy.* They understand the art of *slow* reading by taking time to read at deeper levels of meaning (Newkirk 2012). They engage students in meaningful discussions revolving around quality selections. They reach deeper levels by teaching the *reader* over the book and helping students think about their own thinking as they read (Serravallo 2010, 3).

4. Excellent teachers *recognize that high-quality student talk heightens teaching.* They are willing to move from a "telling mode" to rich language that supports, instructs, and engages learners (Johnston 2004, 2012). They know overreliance on telling may "rob children of the opportunity to take responsibility for their own skills and strategies" (Taylor, Peterson, Pearson, and Rodriguez 2002, 278). They view teacher-supported language as a scaffold to gently nudge students in making discoveries.

5. Excellent teachers *use written tools to support learning over time.* Anchor charts, or coconstructed visual references, make students' thinking public and permanent through "questions, quotes, ideas, and big understandings displayed throughout the room" (Miller 2008, 61). These concrete references "leave tracks of their thinking through writing and drawing so they can take it public" (Harvey and Goudvis 2008, 18). They value students' thinking and offer many opportunities for them to verbalize that thinking.

6. Excellent teachers *explicitly teach and support proficient reader strategies.* Think-aloud is our "instructional bread and butter" as we "let children in on one of the best-kept secrets of human cognition—what we think about as we read" (Keene and Zimmerman 2007, 20). We acknowledge teacher expertise by recognizing that

thoughtful discussions require skillful teaching that cannot be scripted (Hammond and Nessell 2011). We also emphasize the key strategies used by proficient readers as suggested by Keene and Zimmerman (2007, 14).

SEVEN KEY METACOGNITIVE STRATEGIES

- monitoring for meaning
- using and creating schema
- asking questions
- determining importance
- inferring
- using sensory and emotional images
- synthesizing

7. Excellent teachers *use a gradual release of responsibility model* (Pearson and Gallagher 1983; Fisher and Frey 2008). They offer more support for new learning and vary this support according to the needs of their students. They promote independence while taking time to build a solid foundation before relinquishing that role to students. They know that student success is paramount and they take responsibility to ensure it is achieved with varying and carefully fading levels of teacher support.

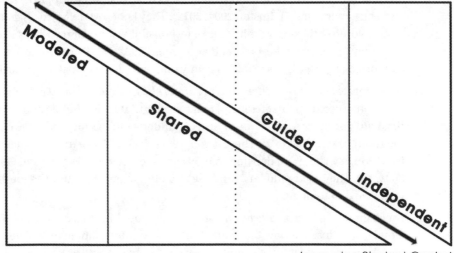

FIGURE 4.6 **Gradual Release of Responsibility Model**

These seven guidelines are the heartbeat of great work. While we may go about achieving these guidelines differently, they are ever-present in our day. These guidelines help us acknowledge that true experts "have a thorough understanding of the reading process and the determination to understand and respond to each child's needs as a reader" (Keene and Zimmerman 2007, 23). This increasing expertise helps us to focus on the simplicity, clarity, and priority that is desperately needed (Schmoker 2011a).

Author Gretchen Owocki beautifully ties these instructional guidelines together:

> *Teachers who do great work create environments for extensive reading and talking about literature. In such classrooms, students read every day throughout the day. They have regular access to texts they can read with understanding, and opportunities to discuss what they are reading with peers who share their interests and questions. Great work recognizes that children learn to read by reading extensively in a variety of meaningful contexts. (email message to author, October 16, 2011)*

Saying No to Bad Work So We Can Say Yes to Good Work and Great Work

Using our guidelines as an instructional GPS, we'll look at teachers who are striving to accomplish two key goals. First, they work diligently to achieve more great work. Second, they understand that this requires eliminating bad work that competes for time. Excellent teachers opt for what will most likely impact student learning and exclude what will not. In other words, they make responsible choices every day.

 SPOTLIGHT TEACHER **Heather Cantagallo**, Grade 4: Pre-Lesson Discussion

Let's begin with Sunapee, New Hampshire, teacher Heather Cantagallo. After nineteen years of teaching, Heather's dramatic transformation began three years ago when she initiated reading workshop and made small-group and side-by-side learning her focus. Her steadfast commitment to students is reflected in her words: "This year [2011–12] after reflecting on the idea of bad work, good work, and great work, I have made a concerted effort to move toward the best work I can do with my students."

This transformation first required her to adjust her schedule. She explicitly teaches routines for meaningful literacy independence using Daily Five (Boushey and Moser 2006, 2009) and uses Fountas and Pinnell benchmark assessment (2010a, 2010b) and independent conferences to assess students' learning needs. Her new schedule rose from a trial and error process.

> I created a weekly schedule for groups and individuals with days/times. Next, I plugged in which students received outside support and counted the number of times they worked with an adult each week. I tweaked my plan to ensure my neediest students had the most support. I gave students a personal schedule and made more tweaks. Finally, I used my parent volunteers to add another opportunity for students to interact with an adult. My best readers currently have five adult interactions each week (with two small-group sessions). My lowest readers have over fifteen interactions each week (with ten small-group sessions).

Heather's success results from her willingness to adjust her day to accommodate her new sense of commitment. She has gradually modified her schedule to meet the needs of students. She knows she can only do her "best work" by putting her goals into action. This requires thoughtful planning and flexibly considering every detail.

To accommodate more small-group and one-to-one time, she decreased whole-class instruction with brief daily focus lessons. These sessions create a community of learners and set the stage for the day. She introduces and reinforces strategies, concepts, and skills using beautiful read-alouds or shared reading and then addresses these learning goals in smaller settings.

Heather knows her students need individual support. She forms flexible small groups based on her interactions in one-to-one conferences and prioritizes struggling students without ignoring the needs of more proficient readers. Heather noticed four

FIGURE 4.7 **Heather uses read-alouds in a focus lesson to introduce key instructional strategies and concepts**

students had difficulty identifying important events in fiction texts during independent conferencing, so she shared with me her four instructional goals for her small-group lesson.

1. Warm Up: Students will complete a word sort to review past words. After working with a partner to create the sort, they will trade sorts for a partner check.

2. Familiar Rereading: Students will whisper-read a brief portion of the story as Heather rotates. She will use this time to listen to a selected child read so she can assess strategy use.

3. Book Lover's Book (BLB): Students will find a favorite line from the story and self-select interesting words to record in their BLB.

4. Informal Discussion: Students will discuss important ideas from the story. They will then work together to write these on a form to sequence key story ideas.

Heather's primary goal was to create a more meaningful and pleasurable reading experience. Therefore, we made simple adjustments to maximize this goal:

- Like many excellent teachers, Heather's desire to give students her best can lead to trying to plan too many activities. Since this can minimize learning, we decided to focus only on identifying important events in fiction texts. Heather is learning that *less can lead to more because it affords the time to move to deeper levels of understanding*.

- Fourth-grade students need time to read silently but Heather can listen to them read without sacrificing these opportunities. Heather will rotate to offer individual attention and listen to students read softly as others read silently.

- We modified Heather's original form to be more interactive (see Figure 4.10). We asked students to select ideas they found relevant first and then initiated an engaging negotiation to narrow those initial ideas through meaningful discussion.

Initial Lesson Based on Our Discussion

Heather knows that instructional goals and reading for meaning and enjoyment are not mutually exclusive. Heather designs this small-group lesson so that her students have a second exposure to the reading selection. Heather begins with time for students to reread their favorite part independently as she rotates. As students read silently, she pauses to listen to individuals read orally, standing behind them for a more informal atmosphere. She looks for evidence of strategy use she can reinforce or teaching points to incorporate into her lesson. Heather knows these first few minutes set the stage for a positive learning experience and offer valuable information about her students. She also knows her first goal is to increase the volume of reading, so every student reads at all times as Heather provides individual support as needed. She then sets a clear purpose for reading using

FIGURE 4.8 **Heather rotates as students read silently to offer feedback and make observations that will inform her teaching**

FIGURE 4.9 **Heather actively engages students in successful learning at all times**

the adapted form based on our discussion. She asks her students about the events in the story, acknowledging every idea while encouraging them to focus on key points. These are recorded on sticky notes to place on the form (see Figure 4.10). Then they identify the most important recorded events and move these to a new column. Dialogue creates a negotiation that celebrates their thinking as we help them to elaborate on initial ideas. She then asks students to write down four key events, offering varied degrees of support to promote independent problem solving. They notice the humor of "ewe" as the lesson closes and she tells them they will look for more examples the next day. She knows teachable moments lead to new opportunities and she is willing to take into account their interests and the responses that rise from the learning activity.

Final Reflection and Future Recommendations

One characteristic that makes Heather an outstanding teacher is that she values each moment in her teaching, reflected by a small clock she uses to ensure students remain on task. Our final debriefing focuses on adjustments she can make in the future.

- **Limit the scope of the lesson.** The modified form places the focus on sharing ideas rather than simply citing the story events. Initiating engaging teacher-supported discussions may be a better expenditure of Heather's time than a second form she had created or additional learning objectives.

- **Use dialogue to enrich student learning.** Heather expertly engages students in discussion, but she can build on this goal in many ways. Asking them to discuss ideas before writing reinforces thinking and offers valuable information about students. It also provides an opportunity to initiate meaningful dialogue to support thinking and writing.

- **Focus on meaning over recall.** Citing events in sequence puts high cognitive demand on recall over comprehension. It can be more effective to acknowledge thinking first, initiate a negotiation of ideas, and then ask students to summarize the big idea using written notes as a supportive tool. Meaning is always the first goal.

- **Use the book to promote ideas and build meaning.** The text is a valuable tool to promote meaning. Heather can encourage students to revisit the text by rereading or discussing ideas. This emphasizes thinking over events while it also affords her valuable information about their thinking during the learning process.

- **Create an enlarged open-ended anchor chart.** Heather will substitute her small chart for an enlarged open-ended version that can be used in other contexts. Sticky notes make it easy to use the chart in small-group or whole-class lessons and they can also be transferred to small-group file folders as anecdotal notes to review later.

Heather uses every second wisely by interacting with students individually or as a group. As students read silently, she listens to individual students read aloud to assess their learning needs or offer scaffolded support. This will maximize her limited time with students while it affords new understandings she can use in planning future lessons. Heather's ability to engage students in a lively discussion makes them active participants so that her role can become more of a supportive one.

FIGURE 4.10 **An open-ended form can provide a meaningful response activity**

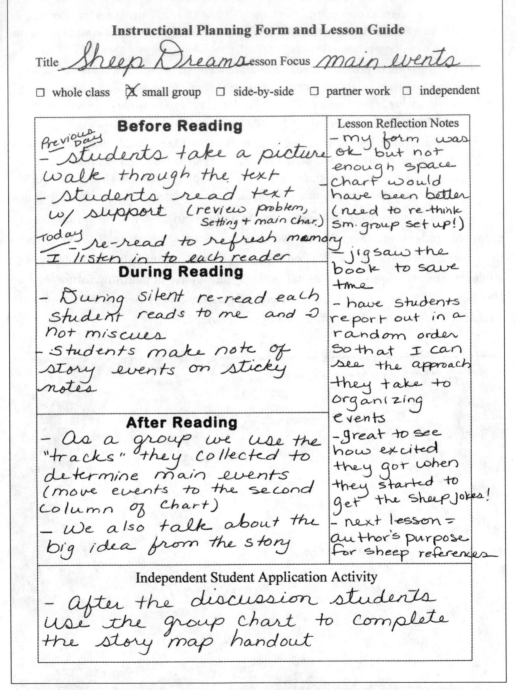

Instructional Planning Form and Lesson Guide

Title _Sheep Dreams_ Lesson Focus _main events_

☐ whole class   ☒ small group   ☐ side-by-side   ☐ partner work   ☐ independent

Before Reading	**Lesson Reflection Notes**
Previous Day - students take a picture walk through the text - students read text w/ support (review problem, setting + main char.) Today - re-read to refresh memory I listen in to each reader	- my form was ok but not enough space chart would have been better (need to re-think sm. group set up!) - jigsaw the book to save time
During Reading - During silent re-read each student reads to me and I not miscues - students make note of story events on sticky notes	- have students report out in a random order so that I can see the approach they take to organizing events
After Reading - As a group we use the "tracks" they collected to determine main events (move events to the second column of chart) - We also talk about the big idea from the story	- great to see how excited they got when they started to get the sheep jokes! - next lesson = author's purpose for sheep references

Independent Student Application Activity

- after the discussion students use the group chart to complete the story map handout

FIGURE 4.11 **Heather reflects on each aspect of the lesson to make adjustments that will enhance her teaching in the future**

Heather uses our first form in this chapter to think about each aspect of her lesson. Reflection helps us consider adjustments that will lead to more great work in the future. She uses the left column to plan her lesson and then evaluates the success of the lesson or consider what she may do next in the right column. She knows these concrete references will offer an instructional guide that can lead to the "best work" she desires.

To help Heather build on what she is already doing well, I suggested expanding on her BLB using Leslie Blauman's BLB approach (2011). This combined view will allow her to add vocabulary and new categories such as a literature log, summary, reflections, and strategies. Not surprisingly, she quickly made this addition.

The ultimate goal of these professional opportunities is that teachers will take ownership of the changes. Heather has learned to value silent reading and gives students many opportunities to practice daily. This was recently confirmed when Rayna wrote, "I can read better in my head than out loud. I wish somehow you could hear me read in my head." Great work has shown Heather how to grant Rayna's wish because it is sometimes as simple as acknowledging students' learning desires. Thank you for listening, Heather!

Celebrate the good work you are already doing while exploring how to make it even better using the Instructional Planning Form and Lesson Guide. Like Heather, we constantly strive to ensure the highest quality teaching. Heather embodies a commitment to students and her knowledge of the reading process. She selects goals based on daily observations, engages students in meaningful literacy, and makes time for targeted support. She balances instruction with time to read for pleasure as defined by Newkirk: "A robust approach to engaged reading embraces both the flow of the "reading zone" [Atwell 2007] *and* strategies for reflection" (2012, 8). Heather knows she doesn't have to choose between her instructional goals and reading for deeper meaning and pleasure. She views them as equally relevant and makes room in her day for both.

Generating an "Instructional Trash Can" to Shift Our Attention to the Seven Guidelines

To begin doing more great work, we must first eliminate all "organizational inefficiency" (Allington 2012a). Excellent teachers don't have more time in their day. They just create a mental "stop doing list" to let go of ineffective practices (Collins 2001). Let's start our own "stop doing list" by looking at some practices that should be reevaluated. We'll begin with a description of a shocking substitute for literacy:

> *They were coloring. Coloring on a scale unimaginable to us before these classroom*
> *tours. The crayons were ever-present. Sometimes, students were cutting or building*

things out of paper (which they had colored) or just talking quietly while sitting at "activity centers" that were presumably for the purpose of promoting reading and writing skills. These centers, too, were ubiquitous, and a great source of pride to many teachers and administrators. They were great for classroom management— and patently, tragically counterproductive. (Schmoker 2001)

The "Crayola Curriculum" illustrates how we sacrifice literacy with time-wasting substitutions. This coloring for the sake of coloring is not the same as brief drawings as a visual representation of thinking. The first is passive while the second is a meaningful tool to leave tracks on our thinking. In the end, it's not *what* we do that matters but *how* we choose to do those things in effective or ineffective ways and for legitimate purposes.

Time is static in that we can't add more, so it makes sense to abandon all "patently, tragically counterproductive" activities. Ten minutes of passive coloring can be spent reading, writing, or talking. We make choices, so let's put another questionable practice under the microscope—worksheets. Sadly, this wolf in sheep's clothing is thriving in far too many classrooms.

I'm not vilifying all worksheets, although most teeter precariously on the edge of bad work. Passive circling, underlining, fill-in-the-blank, coloring, and cut-and-paste cannot substitute for our seven guidelines. Varied excuses are cited such as ease, grades, access, or even parent desire. We may need a national buddy support system where "professionals don't let professionals abuse worksheets" (Schmoker 2009, 526).

So let's rise to the challenge by refusing publisher advice. An instructional trash can allows us to abandon practices that undermine our efforts by eliminating anything *trivial, tedious,* or *thoughtless.* I'm an advocate for differentiated professional growth, or starting where teachers are. For some teachers, this may mean a slow transition from overreliance on a reading program as we eliminate anything that wastes valuable time. To do this, I model how to selectively use or modify forms with a higher purpose in mind.

FIGURE 4.12 **The Danger Zones of Passive Learning**

Saying No to Mindless Worksheets So We Can Say Yes to *Worthsheets*

Two worksheet samples commonly used to teach the recommended skill of *-ing* words are shown. In the first, students identify animals and *-ing* words (*running*). In the second, a word is matched to an animal. The fact that little thought is needed to do these worksheets should sound a global warning alarm for impending bad work on the horizon.

In the revised form, the topic (animals) and suggested goal (-*ing* words) is intact, but the purpose is dramatically altered. The text was too difficult for some students, so we gathered animal texts at varied levels and put them in a basket. This widened our reach since each child now has access to a high-success text and choice is offered.

The skill (-*ing*) is now a vehicle for discussing the text rather than the end goal. Words are not merely lifted from print but students are encouraged to use words, pictures, or schema to make personal discoveries. There are no "right" answers and the

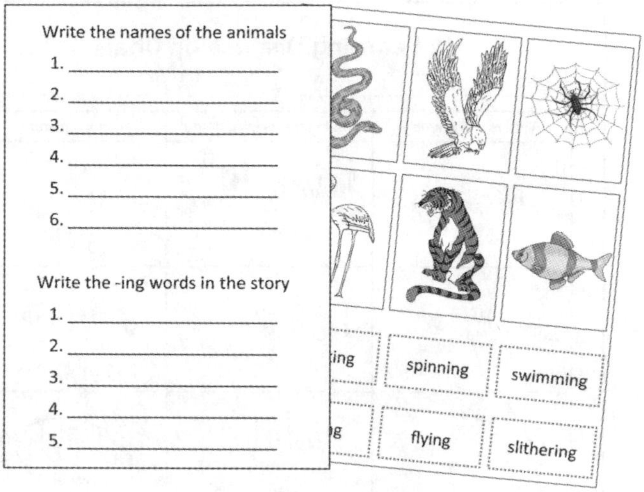

FIGURE 4.13 **Passive seatwork wastes valuable time that can be used in far more productive ways**

skill is elevated to a detour along a meaningful path rather than the final stopping point.

Second-grade teacher Julie Grupczynski from Rochester, Minnesota, helped me initiate this process by reviewing -*ing* words (see Figure 4.15). The whole-class chart provides a reference as a starting point to apply learning in meaningful contexts in varied settings.

We then formed a small group for more targeted support. I modeled the thinking on one page (What is the animal doing?), letting the discussions rise from the experience. Students then read an expert page of their choice silently as I rotated. Next, each child described their page and added an event of their choosing to the chart. They didn't just lift words but interpreted ideas (What are you noticing? What else may be happening?).

Our student experts then introduced this activity in the classroom, showing their classmates how to read the page and add interesting information to the "worthsheet." This reinforced learning and raised confidence for these students by giving them a central role that engaged them at a deeper level.

Every student then selected an animal book from the basket and worked alone or with a partner to complete the form (see Figure 4.14). Varied texts addressed the range of reading needs and took interest into account in a way that is impossible with a one-size-fits-all book. It also built in more time for us to rotate so that we could support their efforts, ask probing questions, or informally assess selected students.

Worthsheets can be a good alternative to traditional worksheets, but we should also consider eliminating the form altogether. In this third-grade class in Mustang, Oklahoma,

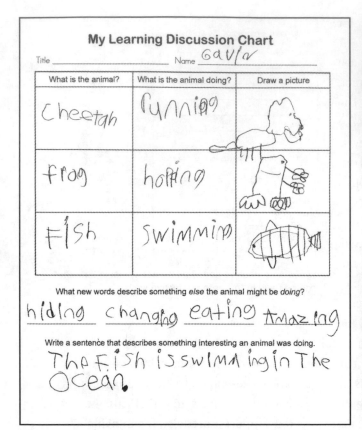

FIGURE 4.14 **An open-ended form can support meaningful reading**

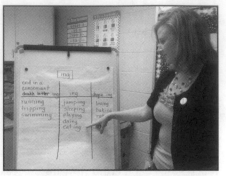

FIGURE 4.15 **Julie introduces a skill during a whole-class focus lesson**

FIGURE 4.16 **The focus lesson is a springboard to apply new learning in appropriate texts**

a graphic organizer was created with three animal categories: Appearance (What do they look like?); Habitat (Where do they live?); and Behavior (How do they act?). Students now work independently to record their ideas on sticky notes and then share and organize these ideas on the chart. A shared anchor chart offers more opportunities to engage students in discussion and student think-aloud than an individual form.

Once again, we returned to a whole-class setting so our experts could demonstrate this activity for their peers. Everyone chose an animal book of their choice and used the sticky notes to record information they found interesting. We rotated to offer individual support that was now feasible because students were all meaningfully engaged in the learning activity with peers. This placed as much emphasis on the *readers* as the *reading*.

Next, students shared and categorized sticky notes on a class display. A new category was added during our discussion—"We aren't sure." Students were actively engaged in a high success experience and we could support them in the context of that experience.

FIGURE 4.17 **Small-group support gives students time to be the expert and reinforces learning**

FIGURE 4.18 **Small groups afford valuable opportunities to learn new strategies through teacher-supported learning**

FIGURE 4.19 **Students apply new learning using sticky notes as the teacher rotates**

Don't be fooled into thinking that passive practice pages are anything more than time-wasters. Shouting a resounding and collective "no" can be exhilarating.

Once we say "no" to activities that are not worth our students' time, we will be able to say "yes" to learning experiences that are far more productive, such as:

- using sticky notes to create a graphic organizer to reference learning
- creating a word wall of interesting vocabulary words with simple illustrations
- writing a coconstructed paragraph about one animal using the graphic organizer
- forming jigsaw groups so students can work together to be the expert of an animal
- letting students research an animal of their choice to create a class book
- letting students become teachers as they share their discoveries with peers

To illustrate these adjustments, see a comparative view on page 88.

Saying No to Technology Without Purpose So We Can Say Yes to Smart Technology

Many teachers have access to a potentially welcome new visitor called SMART Board (names vary). We should take advantage of technological advances (Reutzel and Cooter 2011; Tompkins 2009). We must, however, use them in *smart* ways so it isn't a worksheet with a plug or technology as an "expensive nonsolution" (Allington 2011, 42).

Dawn Poyndexter, first-grade teacher in Tulsa, Oklahoma, uses a SMART Board as an instructional tool to

FIGURE 4.20 **Student-created sticky notes are organized on a class chart**

COMPARISON OF PASSIVE WORKSHEETS AND MEANINGFUL ALTERNATIVES	
Highly Suspect Worksheet Activities	**Reading and Writing Alternative Activities**
fill in missing letters (initial, medial, final)	complete a word sort or use magnetic letters to create words based on your goals
complete a sentence matching a picture	create a cut-up sentence from a story that students can read, rearrange, and reread
circle the correct grammatical word	use real reading and writing to identify these concepts based on learning goals
circle a picture to match a word/sentence	summarize important learning and create a simple drawing to support a discussion
select the right inflectional ending	draw attention to specific examples using authentic reading and writing samples
use a picture to fill in the missing word	draw attention to the illustrations and pictures in books and discuss their relevance
fill in the correct word for verb tense	write a story and use this as a teaching opportunity to address these concepts
arrange sentences in sequential order	complete a real task (make a sandwich) to sequence events and create a class book
almost any silly worksheet activity	read real books and write about real topics with teacher support and feedback

FIGURE 4.21 **Dawn's students share their ideas as she rotates to support and extend their thinking.**

introduce or preview new material for a successful first reading. She draws attention to key words and concepts, and sets a purpose for reading. She offers additional scaffolded support before students read a newsmagazine. Her supportive overview allows them to apply learning with a partner as she encourages them to discuss the words and pictures. Dawn rotates as they work, knowing valuable opportunities are lost behind the teacher's desk. Her students are engaged in meaningful reading and she can offer varied levels of support to ensure success at all times for all students.

Saying No to Scripted Programs So We Can Say Yes to Professional Judgment

Now let's look at our second form of the chapter to see how teachers use their professional judgment to make instructional decisions. Excellent teachers insist on using programs responsibly by abandoning anything patently, tragically counterproductive. "There is no program, no recipe, no prescription that will supersede the power of a well-informed and caring teacher" (Keene and Zimmerman 2007, 31).

SPOTLIGHT TEACHER **Nita Wood**, Grade 3: Pre-Lesson Discussion

Nita Wood, third-grade teacher in Mustang, Oklahoma, blends twenty-four years of experience with the flexible use of a basal program. She uses it to identify instructional skills during the first semester, but then uses it selectively as an instructional tool during the second semester. Nita masterfully blends her professional knowledge with publisher suggestions. She knows her judgement is key.

We began by evaluating the suggested publisher activities. Nita then selected the proposed skill of evaluating the author's purpose. She knows students need this skill, but also acknowledges that the three passive worksheets provided will do little to elevate their learning. As a knowledgeable professional, she insists on the most effective ways to accomplish her instructional goal. She cannot accomplish this by blindly accepting every suggestion, particularly those that are counterproductive to great work.

We discussed how Nita could teach this skill through reading and writing. She wanted to incorporate anchor charts and use independent reading to meaningfully apply learning at easier levels. We knew the anchor chart would support a variety of settings, including independent reading. She wanted to initiate learning through a whole-class text with time for students to practice learning in independent self-selected texts. She knew this would more effectively illustrate the author's purpose since they could apply learning in varied contexts and texts.

Initial Lesson Based on Our Discussion

Nita used the suggested text, *Tops and Bottoms* (Stevens 1995), because she knew this Caldecott Honor book would engage students. Her anchor chart will help them to identify the author's purpose with examples (proof) to defend their thinking. She wants the chart to be flexible enough to add new ideas from additional selections so she can reinforce learning. She knows revisiting this skill only intermittently is inadequate.

FIGURE 4.22
Nita analyzes suggestions in a teacher's guide to ensure that students are consistently engaged in meaningful learning

Instructional Transformation through Professional Decision-Making

Initial Instructional Description	Suggested Learning Activities	Type

• Prediction
 	
• Author's Purpose
 	
• Context Clues
	• Teacher Read Aloud
	  linking authors
	  purpose
		A

	• Pre-teach vocabulary	A
	• Author's Purpose ✶	W
	• Vocabulary Sentence	W
	• Vocabulary Context Clues	W
	Type: worksheet (w) activity (a)	

Personal Instructional Description	Two Personal Instructional Goals

• Limit the teacher read
  aloud to make room for
  student reading.
• Change sequence web
  during or after reading
✶ Anchor Chart
  • Author's Purpose
• Partner work- vocabulary
  cards
	• Make an open ended
	  anchor chart
	  (mixed grouping)
	• Main Idea / Author's Purpose

	• Jigsaw vocabulary
	  with group review
	  card.

How has your role as professional decision-make changed you as a teacher?

• Teach vocabulary during or after reading.

• Use real world skills.

✶ Extension Activity: Students create another Authors Purpose chart for our hallway using their "Self-Selected Books." ✶

Nita makes pleasurable reading her first goal. After modeling learning about the author's purpose, she asks students to share their ideas using the anchor chart. She knows dialogue is valuable, so she encourages them to verbalize their thinking with others. As students share ideas, she asks thoughtful questions and probes for more information using the story as a tool (Why do you think so? Where did you see that? How can you prove your thinking?). She also uses the story to model this thinking with specific examples.

FIGURE 4.23 **Nita creates a meaningful alternative activity to teach author's purpose**

FIGURE 4.24 **Small-group opportunities allow students to apply new learning with support**

FIGURE 4.25 **Nita gradually relinquishes responsibility as students apply learning using independent texts**

A whole-class activity allows Nita to introduce new learning using an engaging story, but she knows some students need more targeted support. She forms flexible small groups using leveled readers that connect the gardening theme of the whole-class text. In this way, Nita can introduce learning using read-aloud as a springboard and then extend that learning in small-group lessons to reinforce her teaching and promote strategy use with a less challenging text. Nita uses many settings to meet individual needs.

Finally, students use their independent texts to identify the author's purpose. They added a new column (combo) to reflect their discovery that an author can have more than one purpose. Again, Nita wanted to engage students in dialogue and then use the texts to support their thinking. She knows that the process of determining the author's purposes and finding evidence to support that thinking through a productive and engaging learning activity is important. She has achieved the great work she knows would have been impossible if she had opted to use the passive forms recommended.

Nita's third-grade colleague, Patty Woods, also adapted a vocabulary suggestion in this unit. While the teacher's guide

FIGURE 4.26 **Knowledgeable teachers opt for engaging literacy activities over passive publisher suggestions**

suggested teaching words *before* reading, Patty knows that most words are best taught in meaningful contexts beyond the earliest grades (Hammond and Nessell 2011). She initiated a jigsaw vocabulary activity after a whole-class selection. Students became the expert of a word in small groups and then taught the word to peers.

Discussions revolving around recommendations in a teachers' guide are worth having. If fidelity to the program is our only goal, then valuable opportunities for these professional collaborations are lost. If there's a more effective way to teach than what is recommended by the publisher, it is our responsibility to do so. We benefit by publishers' suggestions, but we must consider whether those suggestions meaningfully engage our students in high-quality literacy tasks that blend research and practice. That's our job—and it's "kid-delity" at it's finest!

Teachers Assuming Instructional Control Through Professional Decision Making

In this chapter, we explored guidelines to support our instructional goals. We saw teachers willingly eliminate activities or practices that waste valuable time and opt for those that have the greatest instructional payoff in terms of student learning. We saw teachers moving toward the great work described by author Jane Olson:

> *Great work is the work that elevates both teacher and learner. It moves the learner forward and enables him to attain new levels of achievement. Great work builds confidence and inspires the learner to reach further, risk more and set higher goals. (email message to author, August 24, 2011)*

The teachers in this chapter made a conscious choice to seize the reigns of instruction by using resources in responsible ways. They place high value on reading, writing, and talking about beautiful literature. "If teachers do not value children's literature, and the possible roles it may play in the reading curriculum, then they will not find time for reading and discussing children's literature" (Serafini 2011, 31).

These seemingly small changes can quickly set an instructional domino effect in motion. Bregman emphasizes that people must take time "to figure out the one and only thing that will have the highest impact and then focus 100 percent of their effort on that one thing" (2011, 248). These teachers put their full concentration toward achieving their one thing and eliminating anything standing in the way of accomplishing it.

Our seven guidelines are based on the principle that students spend the day engaged in authentic literacy rather than the "stuff" that simply saps our time and energy. "Students could and should be reading and writing in class on average at least four to five times as much as they are now. If they did, the effect would be breathtaking" (Schmoker 2011b, 69).

It is worth emphasizing that Schmoker's recommendation to multiply authentic literacy engagement is not limited to our most proficient readers. Author and special education teacher, Kelly Davis, reminds us to create an inclusive culture:

> All *students are general education students* first. *Like their peers, our most tangled readers deserve more time with high-interest reading and writing experiences and meaningful talk revolving around those experiences. Through these experiences, we are able to offer both opportunity and support. (email message to author, March 15, 2012)*

With each tick of the instructional clock, we can lift students to great heights of learning or hold them cognitive hostages in an instructional dead end. Great work doesn't happen by chance. It's a conscious choice we make using a new mind-set that forever alters our thinking. Questions can drive that thinking, as illustrated by Lesley Scheele:

> *I can't stop asking myself after each lesson: What was bad? What was good? What was great? This constant question has pushed me to think and reflect more than I ever have. (email message to author, September 20, 2011)*

If we could all ask these same simple but critical questions and then base the bulk of our day addressing our seven literacy guidelines, our teaching would most certainly change in dramatic and permanent ways. The answers to such questions will undoubtedly lead to new directions that can substantially enhance our teaching. Any new directions that will affect student learning in positive ways are certainly worth exploring. And our students are worth that effort.

CHAPTER 5

Reframing Assessment as a Professional Tool to Promote Instructional Change

66 *Teachers who do great work spend more time carefully listening to their students in order to teach and assess their literacy needs and strengths. Listening is a simple, yet powerful, way to do the work that really matters."*

(Kouider Mokhtari, email message to author, October 3, 2011)

The teacher signals and students quickly disperse. Suddenly, the room is ablaze with the low hum of activity. I become a willing outsider looking in, opening my mind to the multitude of sights and sounds unfolding before me. I hear excited discussions blending into timid conversations. I see steadfast confidence amid dark clouds of confusion. I hear voices rise in rhythmic cadences merging with laborious hesitations. I record my personal wonderings as I slowly meander, confident my rushed scribbles will convey new insights. I envision the grand possibilities ahead, and I am exhilarated to discover what waits around the next bend!

This could describe the range of learners in any classroom when we are willing to watch and listen. We may see and hear either conversations that bring texts to life with vivid examples or a regurgitation of trivial details. We may see and hear either self-assured engagement or excessive dependence on others. We may see and hear either expressive oral reading with a dramatic flair or word-by-word renditions devoid of meaning.

Excellent teachers employ *watchful listening* habits whenever students are present. We detect opportunities invisible to others, intuitively attending to precise moments. We zero in as students actively engage in learning, sifting through discrete details to uncover new understandings. We are "careful observers, constantly making decisions about how to use information we gather to inform our instruction" (Johnson and Keier 2010, 180).

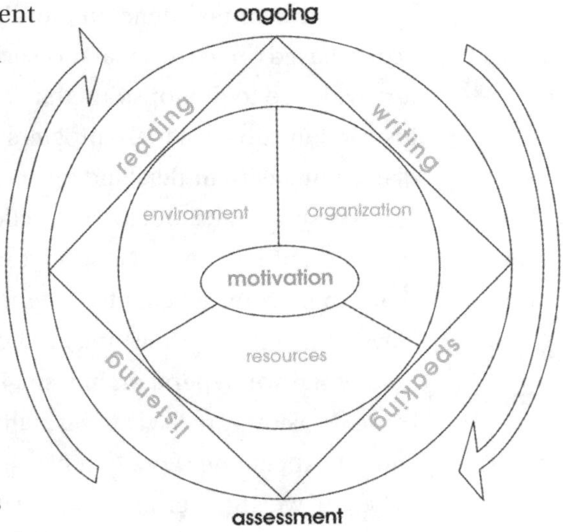

Teachers doing more great work use assessment to inform instruction, but *they* also benefit from this process. They view assessment inseparably interweaved with instruction as a potent transformative tool that can change students and themselves as learners. They use daily watchful listening to pose thoughtful questions about their own instructional approaches to generate a guide that potentially leads to new understandings.

I use the term *potentially* deliberately. While effective assessment practices raise the possibility of this transformative process, it does not guarantee it. *What* we do has little impact unless we are cognizant of *how* to do those things in the most effective ways and for legitimate purposes. Reading records without analysis to shed light on the "next step" is of little consequence because they will be of limited benefit to students.

FIGURE 5.1

In this chapter, we will explore this dual nature of assessment within meaningful contexts. We will see how daily learning experiences offer both an instructional and professional springboard to improved instruction. We will see teachers employ daily habits of watchful listening and act upon the valuable information they use in learning opportunities that abound. We will see teachers take personal responsibility for their day-to-day choices using two overarching questions (note the emphasis on *our* role):

1. How will this knowledge impact how *I* approach learning for this student?

2. How will this knowledge make *me* a more effective teacher as a result?

Broadening Our Assessment Point of View to Elevate Instructional Decision Making

The question then becomes, what assessments in an unlimited pool of options will best support this transformative process? Many assessments can inform practice if viewed as only one measure strengthened by multiple sources while others inadvertently lead to bad work due to misinterpretation or because they don't warrant the time requirements. "In busy classrooms, we just don't have time anymore to collect data that isn't absolutely essential to helping readers improve" (Opitz, Ford, and Erekson 2011, ix).

Some schools spend an inordinate amount of time collecting nonessential data. Scores based on narrow markers such as speed are used to make weighty decisions with no "evidence to demonstrate that if teachers use DIBELS [or variations] to shape their instruction, kids will make progress on some measure of something that really matters, like reading with understanding or comprehension" (Allington and Pearson 2011, 71).

We should account for instructional *and* assessment time. A sign in Albert Einstein's Princeton office stated "Not everything that counts can be counted, and not everything that can be counted counts." Yet the magnitude of decisions based on narrow markers leave some schools drowning in a bottomless data pit.

When we depend on any single measure to make decisions about our students, those decisions are likely to be faulty. From standardized tests to classroom grades, we cannot expect one score to reflect a child. "If someone proposed combining measures of height, weight, diet, and exercise into a single number to represent a person's physical condition, we would consider it laughable" (Guskey 2011, 18). Yet that is precisely what we do in schools every day.

Formative assessment is the basis of successful teaching and can lead to dramatic increases in student achievement (Black and Wiliam 1998, 2010; Dirksen 2011; Heritage 2007; Wormeli 2006). At least in part, this is due to our ability to assume an interactive role by offering feedback to reinforce or support learning in meaningful contexts or in the heat of the instructional moment. Good assessment touches future learning for students primarily because it gives teachers the knowledge to make the best choices in the future.

I am not suggesting summative assessment is unimportant, but that an interactive process influences teaching in ways numerical data cannot. Formative assessment is not designed to label students but to alter the trajectory of their success. It engages us more deeply in the instructional process because it occurs within the context of learning rather than as something else we do. Formative assessment can take place in the context of the learning day so it often requires no extra time and allows us to offer immediate feedback.

Formative assessment emphasizes "knowledge driven" rather than "data driven" schools (Thomas 2011). These sensible assessments have a broader, more potent purpose in that they are designed to improve both learning and teaching (Opitz, Ford, and Erekson 2011, 7). To emphasize this, we draw from the first three standards for the assessment of reading and writing (International Reading Association and National Council of Teachers of English 2010):

- The interests of the student are paramount in assessment.
- The teacher is the most important agent of assessment.
- The primary purpose of assessment is to improve teaching and learning.

As we consider classroom assessments that can support this potent transformative process, we begin by reallocating our time as described by author Kelly Boswell:

Teachers may mistakenly think that long hours correcting papers or grading mean-ingless homework packets will produce great work, but great work occurs when children are present. When teachers take the time to listen and observe students as they read, write, think, and talk, they begin a journey toward great work. If we want to reach new heights as teachers, we need to strive to learn all we can about how children learn best. (email message to author, September 1, 2011)

Classroom Assessments Designed to Both Inform *and* Transform Instructional Practices

We do use each moment children are present to strive to learn all we can about how they learn best—and then act on that knowledge in professionally responsible ways. Daily formative assessments influence instructional outcomes *and* change us as teachers. In this chapter, we will see teachers use assessment to inform *and* transform instruction.

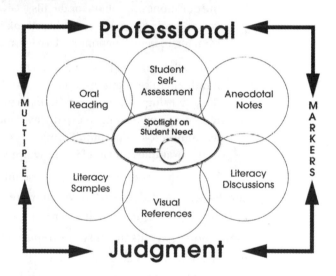

FIGURE 5.2 **Powerful Informal Assessment Options**

Oral Reading: We need daily opportunities to listen to students as they actively engage in reading. These experiences include performances such as readers' theatre, rotating during small-group or independent reading, one-to-one conferencing, or meaningful oral reading that rises from the learning activity. We learn a great deal about students as we listen, although oral reading does not preclude the role of silent reading.

Anecdotal Notes: Anecdotal notes are written notations that help us notice things that may be otherwise invisible. Concrete references over time help us uncover patterns, notice strengths, or explore areas of need. These may be created on the fly with sticky notes on a clipboard, or intentional references in recorded forms. Long-term reference collections placed in a notebook or student folder allow us to connect past and current learning.

Student Self-Assessment: Students need opportunities to assess their personal growth through written or oral experiences. These opportunities are about more than assessing oneself as a learner. They are also about identifying how one can grow as a learner. We want them to ask, "What do I know about myself as a learner? How can I use what I know to grow as a learner?" These are worthy questions at any age.

Literacy Samples: Authentic learning samples create an instructional template of a child's learning journey. Samples reflect where students have been, where they are at that time, or where they need to go. Carefully selected over time, learning artifacts help us to make instructional decisions. They offer a pertinent glimpse of students as real-life learners and illuminate patterns that can support these choices.

Literacy Discussions: Valuable assessment rises from text-based discussions in whole-class, small-group, or side-by-side learning. We glean insight from conversations with students if we listen deeply by reflecting on the thinking that led them there and asking questions or probing for details ("Give me an example"; "Tell me more"; "How do you know?"). When we make their thinking public, we can reinforce or stretch that thinking in new directions and we learn more about our students in the process.

Visual References: The magnitude of assessments that rise from daily learning make it difficult to see patterns. Spreadsheets are increasingly popular, but often focus on data that simply relegates students to numbers. More useful visual references include recording oral reading to explore evidence of strategy use, creating a visual display of learning across time, or initiating record keeping through written reference tools such as the examples provided in this chapter.

Embedded in active learning, these informal assessment components work in concert (or even simultaneously). We may create a written record (anecdotal notes) of oral reading and use this to create a visual reference. This interplay between varied assessment sources avoids the misinterpretation that comes from relying on any single measure. Triangulation can uncover patterns or inconsistencies "to illuminate, confirm, or dispute what you learned through your initial analysis" (Boudett, City, and Murnane 2010, 90). We pull from every available source of information, but we pay particular attention to these components because they rise from real reading and writing events.

Let's explore this process using our first reflection form in this chapter based on a collaboration with kindergarten and first-grade teachers at Mustang Elementary in Mustang, Oklahoma. These teachers know each second counts for their beginning readers and that daily learning experiences set the stage for all that follows. They know students suffer the consequences of wasted time, so they make responsible choices every day.

At the top of the form, teachers identified potential assessment markers of bad work they want to avoid and assessment markers that reflect good work or great work. Selected practices they want to initiate are listed at the bottom with a description of how they will accomplish them, along with a projected implementation date. This open-ended form personalizes their choices, making it easy for each teacher to establish priorities.

The form makes it easy to see ineffective practices to alleviate (bad work), quality approaches in place to celebrate (good work), and effective additions to accommodate (great work). Lasting change occurs with smaller increments so initiating a goal thoughtfully with one student in the beginning will form good assessment habits at deeper levels over time. The form is a quick visual reference of long-term assessment goals as a menu of options to pull from all year.

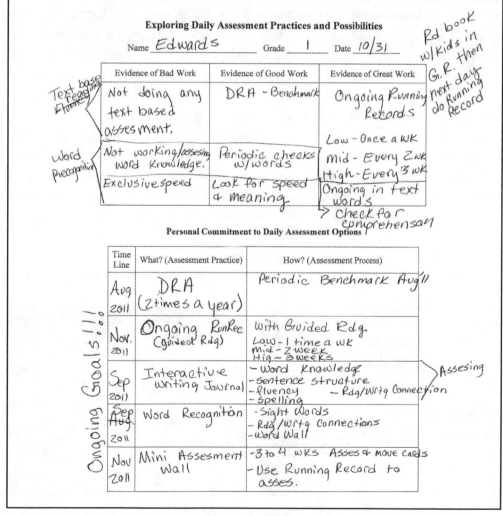

FIGURE 5.3 **First-grade teacher Brittany Edwards explores daily assessment options that will inform her teaching**

SPOTLIGHT SCHOOL Mustang Elementary Teachers Use Interactive Writing Journals

After Mustang Elementary kindergarten teachers Jamie Khosravi, Jaci Wolf, Chelsea Otey, and Megan Broderick completed our assessment form, they decided to begin with interactive writing journals. An interactive journal is a side-by-side shared writing activity combining teacher modeling and support. A student-generated sentence is coconstructed with support to explore sounds, words, or print concepts. This high-success activity engages a child in pleasurable reading and writing. It also lends itself to on-the-spot decision making by combining all of our assessment components in one activity.

Initially developed for first graders in Reading Recovery (Clay 1985), it is easily adapted for struggling learners at any grade. A written message generated by the student promotes alphabetic knowledge *and* print concepts rather than relinquishing learning to twenty-six weeks of letter-a-week drudgery. We can't withhold the very opportunities we so freely offer our most proficient readers. We must view all children as highly capable readers and writers and support them in reaching that achievable goal.

The child generates and records a sentence at the bottom and the top is a practice area for sound boxes, words, and letters. The sentence is written word by word with support and the child rereads after each new word is added. Carlee is still learning letters but we can reinforce known letters in her name (*C, a*) with a new letter (*n*) in a repeated sentence "I can." This allows us to teach letters, sounds, and words simultaneously.

Professionally supportive nonthreatening collaborations ensure a common approach based on high-quality learning. Doing a strategy ineffectively isn't much better than not doing it at all, so shared dialogue is critical—"a strategy is just a tool that teachers can use at

FIGURE 5.4 **An interactive writing journal offers a high-success, teacher-supported literacy experience**

FIGURE 5.5 **The interactive writing journal actively engages students in meaningful reading and writing**

different levels of effectiveness" (Marzano 2011/2012, 89). We need to opt for the highest level of effectiveness to maximize the impact of time expended.

Jamie, Jaci, Chelsea, and Megan are learning how to use interactive journals for their beginning, developing, and advanced learners by adjusting the complexity of the message. They do not feel threatened without a script because they know that *being present in the moment* requires noticing the signs and then trusting their students to point the way. These "noticings" can lead to powerful new teaching experiences.

Jamie Khosravi conducts an interactive journal activity with a kindergarten student. She has developed a heightened awareness and insatiable sense of curiosity. She wants to understand this child as a reader and writer and she knows the smallest details can signal how to help this child grow. Jamie's princess outfit is a visual reminder to her students not to interrupt her important work at the learning table. Interruptions diminish our teaching and send a message that this time is not valuable. We need organizational structures that make room for targeted instruction and promote student independence.

FIGURE 5.6 **Dialogue revolves around creating high-quality learning experiences**

FIGURE 5.7 **Jamie modifies an interactive writing journal activity to meet the unique needs of her kindergarten students**

Jamie illustrates how interactive journals have transformed her teaching:

Now I can teach students writing and phonics skills one-on-one or in small groups. My students write independently and use creative spelling without direct instruction in daily writer's workshop. The interactive journal helps me bring their writing experiences full circle by helping them use correct spelling and sentence structure with immediate feedback as they write. They can also apply what they learn during interactive journal in independent reading and writing. A child recently asked if I could remember how to spell a word we spelled together in his journal so he could spell it correctly during writer's workshop. When I asked if he thought he could spell it without me, his response was "Yeah, if you just give me the boxes and chips I can spell anything." I have seen students gain confidence and pride in their work. They love coming to the teacher table to learn new skills and improve on previous skills. They always ask if they can use their interactive journal. I have become more confident in teaching them to read and write in small groups and I know that our time together is beneficial.

FIGURE 5.8 **Jamie briefly reinforces high-frequency words individually on a daily basis**

FIGURE 5.9 **Kindergarten students practice sight words in their personal word wallets with a peer**

Jamie knows that potent transformation doesn't end when she leaves the activity. She uses what she learns as a springboard to reinforce and extend student learning. Her "word necklace" makes it easy to practice words throughout the day. She also created personal "word wallets" to house each child's known words ("Words I Know") and words in progress ("Words I Need to Practice"). She knows that peer collaboration can maximize the benefits of these smaller settings by providing repeated exposure.

Kindergarten and first-grade teachers came to various conclusions after working with interactive journals:

- "I notice more confidence and greater gain for my first graders than any approach I've used. Many have told me interactive journal is their favorite activity."
- "I notice students make more self-corrections. As I result I have placed 'boo boo' tape [a white tape to correct spelling] in a central location to use at will."
- "I notice more confidence because we correct a word immediately. Reading a sentence they vested time and effort in makes the reading more meaningful."
- "I notice a huge difference in my small groups. I have always done guided reading, word work, and writing in small groups but now I do all three in one."
- "I notice growth as the year progresses. Working in small groups or individually lets me observe each child's thinking process as they write."

Assessing Students' Oral Reading

We can amass rich information as we listen to students read. Our spotlight teacher will demonstrate an activity using five of our six assessment components in combination: oral reading, self-assessment, anecdotal notes, literacy discussions, and visual references.

SPOTLIGHT TEACHER **Patty Woods**, Grade 3: Initial Knee-to-Knee Reading Teaching Activity

Patty Woods is a third-grade teacher in Mustang, Oklahoma. In just five years, she knows that professional learning is a priority, so she is excited to initiate knee-to-knee reading. We used independent texts to address the wide range of readers but wanted the activity to be flexible enough to incorporate other instructional goals. We decided to start with her current goal of expressive, fluent reading. We began by modeling the procedure as we sat knee-to-knee, facing each other with a personal text. We explained to students that we had selected and practiced a favorite part to read with fluency, and we reviewed characteristics of fluent readers. We explained that we would read a brief selection with expression and meaning and our partner would point out something we did effectively in the form of a compliment. I read as Patty listened and then she complimented me using the book as a resource (*I like the way your voice got loud—it helped me understand how the character was feeling*). Next Patty read to me and I complimented

FIGURE 5.10 **Students use independent texts to apply learning goals during knee-to-knee reading**

her (*Your voice changed when you used describing words so I could visualize the setting*). We briefly recorded our compliments on a chart to revisit later, drawing attention to the specific examples. We encouraged students to add more to the chart (*you picked an interesting book, you went slower and faster, you really showed emotion*). Students then identified and practiced their personal selection. This independent self-selected text ensured success and created an engaging and authentic opportunity to revisit and practice reading with a purpose. As they read silently, we rotated. Next, they sat knee-to-knee with a partner and took turns reading and complimenting as we rotated. Patty's students actively engaged in a meaningful learning activity that afforded her time for watchful listening. She was able to explore fluency while recognizing that fluency does not ensure reading with meaning even for proficient readers (Applegate, Applegate, and Modla 2009).

Patty Woods: Broadening Knee-to-Knee Reading

To explore other ways of using knee-to-knee reading, we made a list of some of Patty's instructional goals. Patty used our final list to create a chart for display.

- question
- strategy
- think-aloud
- visual image
- language
- summary
- key detail
- character
- setting
- prediction
- main event
- schema
- confusion
- vocabulary

Patty introduced the chart to her students and explained they had already learned some goals while others will be discussed later. The chart aroused their curiosity while establishing a purpose. Patty had already introduced self-questioning so this was a good starting point. After a brief review, she explained that they would use this strategy in knee-to-knee reading. She showed them how to select a brief, complete idea and modeled how to listen and then ask a question that can be answered. She rotated as students took turns listening and questioning (*Why do you like that character? What kind of lizard is that?*). Students often looked back to find an answer and she encouraged them to read brief portions orally to reinforce a response. Patty listened as they applied this strategy using varied high-interest texts. She was excited to explore new instructional goals using her chart during the year.

FIGURE 5.11 **Patty introduces a new instructional goal for knee-to-knee reading**

Patty Woods: Using Watchful Listening as a Professional Tool

One thing that makes excellent teachers stand out is their ability to develop a stance of "student-aware teaching" (Tomlinson 2008). Patty needs daily time to take a closer look as students engage in literacy. These opportunities help her use what she sees and hears to establish instructional goals. In the hustle and bustle of our day, we need quiet moments side-by-side as students engage in literacy for these watchful listening opportunities. Being present in the moment means taking time to ponder the possibilities.

I asked Patty to share how this experience had transformed her teaching:

FIGURE 5.12 **Patty rotates to listen in as students apply learning in their personal texts**

- "One of my struggling readers found it hard to listen to his partner read from a chapter book. I will match him with a partner who has a picture book."

- "Some students had trouble asking a question so I know they need more modeling. Listening to them helped me think about forming small groups to teach this."

- "I noticed some students read fluently but they still struggled with listening comprehension. I can pay more attention to that during whole-class read-aloud time."

- "Some students are still reading word by word in a too-hard book. I need to review the characteristics of fluent readers and how to choose a just-right book."

> Doing the knee to knee process helped me as a reader and helped me learn more as a reader. I think that we should be partnered with kids who we normally we don't hang out with to learn more about them as a reader.

FIGURE 5.13 **Fifth-grader Hannah Cooney shows knee-to-knee is also relevant in the upper grades**

- "It was hard for some students to find an answer that wasn't right there. I can work on this in my small groups and help them search for and respond to questions."

- "One of my best readers read so fast he missed words that changed the meaning. I need to help him slow down and really think about what he's reading."

- "I want to help my students explain the answer in their own words instead of just reading it again. I'm going to add summarization next to teach this."

Patty and I continued to explore modifications such as generating a question for their own reading to give a partner as a purpose for listening. A child who has difficulty sharing ideas can read to Patty before the activity so she can help the child generate a question. Patty can support this learning in read-aloud, small groups, or conferences. We also discussed using the chart as a menu of options so students can self-select a strategy.

We found that students' feelings about knee-to-knee reading were also positive:

- "I can focus on what my buddy is reading better."
- "It helps me to be a better listener."
- "My partner knows I am listening and focusing on what they are saying."
- "We can give more expression because we have our partner's attention."

🔦 SPOTLIGHT TEACHER

Nita Wood, Grade 3: Adapting Knee-to-Knee for Writing

We first met Patty's third-grade colleague, Nita Wood, in Chapter 4. Knee-to-knee is easily adapted to writing using brief drawings as a guide. If you are concerned about utilizing drawing even after students have learned to read and write well, research does not bear this out. For example, Roam expresses concern that the educational system views pictures as training wheels to discard once we learn to read: "Pictures are the part of thinking that provides us with guidance and direction. It's the 'big picture' that lets us see where we're going. Pictures aren't training wheels; *pictures are the front wheel*" (Roam 2011, 22). Student-created quick draws offer a rich tool for writing and talking.

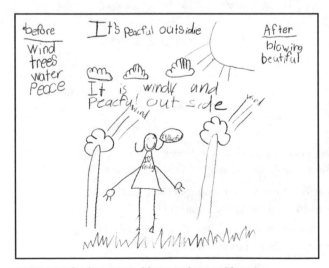

FIGURE 5.14 **Student-created knee-to-knee writing plan**

FIGURE 5.15 **Nita listens in as students share their knee-to-knee writing plan**

Informal Assessment and Instructional Planning Record

Name _Nita Wood_   Grade 3ʳᵈ   Dates _11/11_ to _11/14_

☒ whole class   ☐ small group instruction   ☐ small group extension   ☒ side-by-side

Brief Lesson Description:
Tri-Fold Pre-writing Plan

What? What do I see or hear? (Observation)	Assessment Reflection
• Students getting stuck on the "Idea." • Students writing great before words.	• More time needed for introduction. • Create an Anchor chart.
So What? What do I think? (Interpretation) • Create an anchor chart with students to Introduce this lesson. • Discuss "Jot Ideas" from their writing folder. • Remind students to write about what they have a passion for.	• Make a <u>class</u> writing plan first. • Model questioning technique (put some of these on the anchor chart.)
Now What? What will I do? (Application) • Repeat lesson. • Create anchor chart. • Create a question chart.	

FIGURE 5.16 **Nita can use her observations to increase the quality of knee-to-knee writing**

Web form 10

Nita and I begin by modeling the thinking as we sit knee-to-knee with a trifolded piece of paper. I wrote my idea at the top with a simple drawing in the center and key words on the left to reflect my initial thinking. I share my idea with Nita and she asks questions ("Is that an ocean?"; "What kind of tree is it?"). Her questions stimulate me to think in more detail and my responses elicit new ideas. I add these new details to my picture with more key words In the third section on the right.

Now it is students' turn. They work independently to record a topic, draw the idea in the center, and add key words. We rotate as they work to initiate watchful listening.

Nita uses our second form of the chapter to consider how to enhance this activity. Nita describes how she used her new goals to make the activity more meaningful:

> To reintroduce the trifold writing plan I asked my students to brainstorm something they have wanted to share and write about. We talked about our JOT LIST in our writing folders and how those ideas are just waiting to be written. They shared some ideas and one student mentioned he wanted to write about Laser Tag. We asked him to make a quick draw on our big chart with a few Before Words he wanted to use in the story. My wonderful students asked great questions: What color are the lasers? Did you have to wear something special to play? What are those squiggly lines? I acted as his scribe in the After Column as students questioned him. We discussed how After Words can help him with his piece. I asked them to visualize what he described. We summarized our procedures and then worked independently on our plan. Their plans were much more personalized this time. The next day we paired off with our reading buddy and shared our plans. Just setting the procedures and giving them time to work and share made for much better writing ideas and more thoughtful questions. We now keep our writing plan in front of us.

FIGURE 5.17 **Nita's students collaborate to create a writing plan**

Nita later shared that she was still not happy with the idea part of the lesson since they had difficulty selecting an idea. To address her concern, she used *Arthur Writes a Story* (Brown 1998). "Students *got* the message immediately. Each day since I have heard a student say something about *not* writing about Planet Smellephint!! It reminds me once again not to leave out picture books. Marc Brown did what I could never do—paint a visual picture of what good writers do and don't do."

Nita is an excellent teacher because she knows beautiful literature that is not tethered to an anthology is central to an effective literacy program. She is an excellent teacher because she is not satisfied to give students *good* work—she knows they deserve *great* work. Nita took ownership of an idea and was empowered to let that idea grow in a trial-and-error process that included her students as they achieved great work together.

Patty and Nita view literacy from a broader perspective. "Reading has become a speed reading contest and divorced from the essence of reading-comprehension" (Rasinski and Hamman 2010, 26). Rasinski implores us to move beyond a narrow view:

> *Great literacy work is authentic and creative work, scaffolded by the teacher to lead to a sense of accomplishment. Great work happens when students rehearse a poem under the guidance of a teacher and read with expression for an audience. Great work happens when students transform a story they have read into a readers theater script to practice and perform for classmates. (email message to author, September 27, 2011)*

Using Intensive Instructional Settings to Maximize the Transformative Process

Patty and Nita demonstrated their transformation in a whole-class setting, but more intimate settings can uncover what is otherwise invisible. Side-by-side learning elevates our growth potential because students become *our teachers* as we watch them actively engage in reading. This builds deeper understandings with a newfound sense of clarity as alternate instructional pathways come into sharper focus. We certainly can't say the same when we reduce students to anonymous blips on a spreadsheet radar screen.

We need individualized approaches in authentic contexts using assessments that rise from real literacy events. On-the-run reading experiences allow us to observe our students in meaningful contexts in ways that align assessment and instruction.

Reading records let us peer into a "window on the reading process" (Goodman 1969, 1973). Capturing and analyzing a record of reading helps us identify independent, instructional, and frustration levels to support text selection. We can also notice strategies the child is using, abusing, or confusing during real reading events. Once we understand students as active strategic readers, we can then begin to make better instructional choices.

 **SPOTLIGHT SCHOOL**

Mustang Elementary Teachers Use Reading Records

First-grade teachers at Mustang Elementary in Mustang, Oklahoma, identified reading records as an assessment goal. They want to view students as real-life readers to align their instructional goals. Cross-grade collaborations generate thoughtful dialogue for a shared perspective that is firmly grounded in literacy as a strategic, active process.

FIGURE 5.18 **Collaboration ensures understanding for taking and analyzing reading records**

FIGURE 5.19 **Nicole Erwin explores strategy use as she takes and analyzes a reading record**

First-grade teachers Connie Sloan, Kelli VanNess, Margaret Harkey, Gayla Holmes, and Brittany Edwards are learning how to use reading records to inform their instruction. They can begin this learning process by taking *and* analyzing a record with one student.

It is not enough to simply *do* reading records. We must also understand how to *use* them thoughtfully in ways that impact teaching *and* learning. First-grade teacher Nicole Erwin uses a reading record to view her students in the context of reading. She knows that analyzing the errors will give her valuable information to use instructionally.

I asked teachers at Mustang Elementary to explain how reading records are transforming their instruction:

- "It helps me find the right texts and I'm more confident I'm making good choices."
- "It helps me make the most of my small-group time."
- "I can instantly review miscues to give immediate feedback."
- "I know what skills each child needs so small groups are more beneficial."
- "I can see common reading errors and what reading strategies they are using."
- "I can see the progress students are making in becoming good readers."
- "I get useful information on my beginning readers I can use right away."
- "It helps me form my small groups with students who have similar needs."
- "I love how easy they are to do and that they give me an instructional level."
- "I can select a teaching point to reinforce something the child actually did."
- "It helps me know if I did a good job in my teaching and what I should do next."

While reading records are a powerful assessment option, we need a warning: *Use flexibly and cautiously*. It is a useful tool to identify independent texts in the zone of actual development and instructional texts in the zone of proximal development (Vygotsky

1978), but it is not a perfect science. Thoughtful analysis should lead to sound hypotheses using gradients of ranges or clusters. This broader, more flexible view alleviates the danger of using levels as a narrow reference of students as readers.

There is also a discrepancy about what constitutes instructional and independent texts. Clay suggests 90–94 percent and 95–100 percent accuracy, respectively (1985), but these references are based on one-to-one settings that may be too high for small groups. "We maintain that the work of guided reading needs to be mostly a habituation of the known, as the next stage in the gradual release is independence" (Burkins and Croft 2010, 32). In these contexts, 95–98 percent and 99–100 percent, respectively, may be a more appropriate reference point (Betts 1946).

As a flexible tool, we must also avoid using reading records to assign books in a classroom or school library. This gross misinterpretation ignores the role of choice and fails to teach students how to select just-right books on their own. As elegantly illustrated in Jennifer Serravallo's quote of assistant principal Dina Ercolano, "Children do not have levels; books have levels" (2010, 175).

It is also worth mentioning that analyzing a reading record for strategy use such as evidence of cross-checking, self-correction, or repetition is critical. Without analysis and interpretation, the record is a meaningless piece of paper. We also learn as much from the process itself, so the person taking *and* analyzing a record stands the most to gain. This is why it is so necessary for classroom teachers to assess their own students rather than to merely relegate this to others. Some things simply require *our* concentrated attention.

SPOTLIGHT SCHOOL Sunapee and Mustang Elementary Use Assessment Walls

Teachers at Sunapee Elementary School in Sunapee, New Hampshire, initiated an assessment wall as a schoolwide collaboration. An assessment wall is a problem-solving tool based on professional discussion and collaboration (Dorn and Soffos 2012). Reading records are used to create a visual display. Color-coded cards reflect grade levels with pertinent information. Names are anonymous to maintain a problem-solving approach.

The assessment wall engages teachers in discussions revolving around students and how we can support them both within *and* across grades. We don't just identify who falls below, on, or above expected ranges, but identify *our* role in

FIGURE 5.20 **Reading specialist Jo Skarin and fourth-grade teachers Heather Cantagallo and Katie Blewitt discuss how to support their readers**

ensuring the success of *all* students represented on the wall. We want to reflect on what we can do to increase or accelerate that placement: How do we challenge students above grade level? How do we support students below grade level? How do we continue progress for students at grade level? The wall makes it impossible to ignore any student because they are always in our view. It also reminds us we may need to double or triple the rate of growth for some students since one-year growth in a year will do little more then maintain the status quo. We photograph the wall at each step to use as a comparison along the way.

The assessment wall as a schoolwide approach lets us visually see all students to increase our awareness of needs at each end of the spectrum. Several large pocket charts are used to create the wall so we can add new information to cards and move them during the year. It should be located in a private area for our eyes only, using it to support our discussions as a flexible tool. The concrete nature of the pocket charts lets us physically touch, feel, and move cards, so a SMART Board is not a suggested alternative. This will also help us to remember that these are real students rather than dots on a nameless grid.

Color-coded cards draw attention to a grade level while visually helping us to consider how to join forces through such approaches as forming cross-grade reading buddies. Every student on the wall is included in our discussions, but we can collaborate to level the playing field for those who are not making expected progress. The wall should focus our discussions on the process of reading with strategy-based conversations. We are instantly aware if students stop progressing at any time as growth expectations change at key points in the year (Sunapee moves a color-coded bull's-eye).

Kindergarten and first-grade teachers at Mustang Elementary in Mustang, Oklahoma, created a miniversion of an assessment wall. A smaller version makes it easy to revisit regularly so they are constantly aware if their students are making progress. This awareness is needed every day, not just at a few intervals throughout the year.

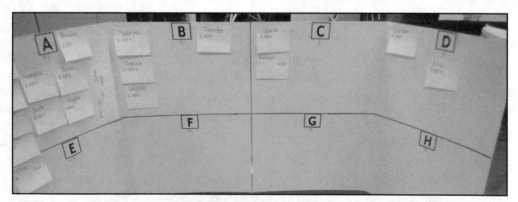

FIGURE 5.21 **The mini–assessment wall makes it easy for teachers to keep track of their students in between the schoolwide assessment wall meetings**

FIGURE 5.22 **Jaci Wolf, Jamie Khosravi, Megan Broderick, Jessica Byars, and Chelsea Otey discuss how to move their readers using the minifolders**

FIGURE 5.23 **Reading specialists Dawn Schuster and Jamie Berry consider where additional student support may be needed**

It can be beneficial to implement an assessment wall at a slower pace. Reading specialists Jamie Berry and Dawn Schuster of Sunset Terrace Elementary in Rochester, Minnesota, support teachers in a slower approach by starting with first and fifth grades. Beginning with willing participants is a good idea in a larger school so we can model and advertise the wall first and it often creates a domino effect as others see the value.

Since a potent transformative process assumes *we* use this information to promote professional change, I captured some thoughtful dialogue revolving around the wall.

- "If we pair our struggling older readers with younger readers as reading buddies, they will have access to easy books they need in nonthreatening settings."

- "We can be really proud of the progress these kids have made. What do you think may have attributed to that? How can we keep doing those things?"

- "We are really seeing growth in these students. What are we doing that has led to this gain so we can consider doing the same for students not making progress?"

- "Can we increase the support options for these kids so we can accelerate their progress faster?"

- "Are we really doing everything we can to make sure these special education students are also successful in our classroom? What else can we do?"

- "We could meet with these students five minutes every day to give them some of the individual support they need. It's a realistic goal to find five minutes daily."

- "What strategies do we need to emphasize for these beginning readers? Can we use some approaches that combine reading and writing?"

- "How can we work together so that we have the same goals for students who are attending multiple instructional settings? Can we find a common ground?"

- "These students have not moved since the last time we met. What could we do or stop doing that could help them make more progress?"

FIGURE 5.24 **Phyllis Cox and Chelsea Carlisle share an anchor chart as teachers collaborate**

FIGURE 5.25 **First-grade teachers Margaret Harkey and Brittany Edwards help Chelsea Carlisle consider how to use an interactive writing journal with her struggling readers**

Sunapee, New Hampshire, fifth-grade teacher Lesley Scheele described how the wall is having an impact on her instruction:

> I never expected the assessment wall to be so enlightening and helpful. When we sit to discuss children with the wall as our backdrop it forces us to be specific and to focus on exactly what each (and every) child needs. We have started to reassess the excitement of "moving" kids up and the pressure to make sure they "move" is amazing. Because of the assessment wall we have implemented some important changes. I have worked one-to-one with one student who was an outlier in comparison to the other fifth graders as one quarter of his targeted instruction and this has made it possible for him to move from a level J to N! The wall has also helped me form homogenous groups for guided reading and targeted instruction, partner "reading buddies" together with like abilities/needs, and identify which groups are ready for more sophisticated book groups. In short, much of my instruction (both whole, small, and one-to-one) has been affected in a positive way.

Lesley and her colleagues are using the wall as one more source of information to inform their teaching. They do not use the wall for one-stop shopping, but view it as a visual tool to support the potent transformative process. This means that it helps them understand students at deeper levels and changes what they do based on what they have learned. Effective instruction is impossible unless we understand who students are and what they need at any given moment. An assessment wall simply gives us one more reference point to make more informed and knowledgeable decisions.

The wall is also a vehicle to generate a common toolbox of high-quality strategies. Mustang Elementary teachers created a strategy wall with four categories: Strategy (What?); Description (How?); In Action (Who?); and Adaptation (What else?). The strategy is identified and described in the first two columns, with photographs of staff "experts" putting it into practice or student samples displayed under "In Action." The last category allows teachers to explore adaptations across grades or content areas. This will offer a visual view of next-step possibilities as we discuss the assessment wall.

Chelsea Carlisle and Phyllis Cox are making many changes in their second-grade classrooms by initiating high-quality flexible small groups with anchor charts they can use in varied settings. They demonstrate how they use anchor charts, using this model for teachers to ask questions or explore adaptations.. The strategy wall grows as new details or examples are added and teachers are encouraged to become a staff expert as they learn.

First-grade teachers Margaret Harkey and Brittany Edwards share their interactive journals with Chelsea Carlisle. They are helping Chelsea consider how this approach can support her students on the assessment wall who need more intensive experiences. Cross-grade professional collaborations broaden the view beyond grade level and open the door to new possibilities. The focus is always on high-quality practices rather than cute ideas, and discussions revolve around the instructional process (thinking) over products (stuff).

SPOTLIGHT TEACHER **Lesley Scheele**, Grade 5: Engages Students in Self-Assessment

Now we'll see how Lesley Scheele's fifth graders in Sunapee, New Hampshire, engage in daily self-assessment using our adapted work categories: Not So Good Work, Good Work, and Great Work. First, they brainstormed examples for each category (Not So Good Work: no reading; Good Work: reading every night; Great Work: read a *ton*!). The examples led to an engaging dialogue that will help students to establish personal goals. This self-assessment makes them accountable for their own success.

The visual provides a common reference point and concrete tool for ongoing discussions. Lesley meets with students regularly to reflect on their successes as they work toward goals and helps them consider whether to modify an existing goal or select a new one (*I need to slow down to read more carefully and do my best work*). This engages students in the assessment process and helps Lesley see where support is needed.

Lesley created a form students complete weekly. Their discussions revolve around specific work samples for even more personalized goal setting. These references increase Lesley's

FIGURE 5.26 **Lesley listens as a student verbalizes her successes and sets new goals**

FIGURE 5.27 **Students put their goals in writing as an ongoing self-assessment reference tool**

Name: *Erin Moynihan*   Awesome Quarter!

Second Quarter: *What kind of work do you do?*

Not So Good Work	Good Work	Great Work	Plan
Not doing you work or not finishing your work	Write and add details to written work	Elaborating on each detail AND Remembering all the parts of an essay (TED)	I need to elaborate a little bit more on some of my writing
Rushing through work and NOT checking work for mistakes	Taking your TIME!	Double checking – making work your best!	Sometimes on big assignments I froget to double check all my work
Spending time GooFING AROUND during work time	Focusing and sitting where you can WORK HARD!	Staying Focused: Having supplies, staying put, working the whole time!	I need to keep working hard like I have been.
Putting off work or PROCRASTINATING	Didn't wait until the last minute	Having a plan – Breaking big assignments down	I should start having a plan Sometimes I froget to have a plan.
Lack of EFFORT - Not quality work!	Trying Hard and Being Confident	EXCELLENT EFFORT - You feel PROUD AND EXCITED!	I always have to remeber to have great effort.
Not Reading :(	Reading EVERYDAY and NIGHT!	READ A TON! (90 mins daily) Getting LOST in a BOOK	I need to keep up the reading. Super!

FIGURE 5.28 **Students reflect on their growth and set new goals with peers using the chart**

knowledge about students and how she can support continued growth. Our ability to act on our understandings is central to a potent transformative process.

Students also have many opportunities to share their goals with peers. Lesley knows a gradual release of responsibility means she will relinquish this role to students.

Lesley reflected on how the chart supports her work:

I am amazed at their ability and eagerness to set goals and work toward "great work"! Now they understand how goals and plans connect to their achievement. They are eager to get rid of what is not working. I've never had a class reflect so insightfully and confidently! It is magic!

Of course, student self-assessment means their perspective is equally relevant:

- Emma: "It helps me understand what to do during workshop time and to see what the teacher expects from you."

- Hannah: "Looking at the chart helps me a lot because I know what would be not so good work, good work and great work for fifth grade."

- Ashley: "When I write something I look up at the chart and think what do I have to put in my writing and how can I make it better?"

- Jake: "It helps me know where I am on the chart and how I could make my work even better."

- Maddy: "I can see where I fall to try to make my work something I'm proud of."

- Matthew: "I can set better expectations for myself."

- Cayelin: "The chart makes me feel great because I want to do great work."

Lesley allows these experiences to flow into new goals. Based on the goal for students to read at home, they created a plan to read during the holidays. Students identified and secured books they planned to read and created a graph to reflect the number of hours they will read. This engages them in goal setting and initiates students in wonderful dialogue about their reading goals. Lesley can also demonstrate her role as a reader by setting her own goals. Lesley describes the process in her words:

My class (including me) made a challenge to read as much as possible between now and the first of the year! We all made "reading plans" and kids figured out when they can read, who can help them find books and time to read. We all went on a book hunt to find the books to read next. You should have seen the kids with their stacks and leaving with backpacks full. The reading plan got them all revved up to build their habits. The form made them think about what they were reading right now, how the book was going, when they thought it would be done, when they planned to read, how often, what their reading goals were for the next seventeen days and what help they needed to meet their goal (help from parents with quiet time, a reminder to take a book on a long car trip, book suggestions from friends/teachers, etc.). They searched my library (with my help), the school library (with librarian's help), and the Lit Lab (with Jo/Deb's help). The kids were so excited and so thoughtful about choices. They thought deeply about what they really want to read next, they were chatting about choices, giving recommendations, and deciding to read the same books to discuss. It was wonderful! When they had their pile they made a list of books and started to read! They each made a bar graph to track the hours they read each day between now and January 1st. I won't allow my kid to say "Oh I was on break, I forgot a book, I didn't read anything . . ." I see it as my primary job to not only instill a love of books but to help my students develop a real "reader's habit."

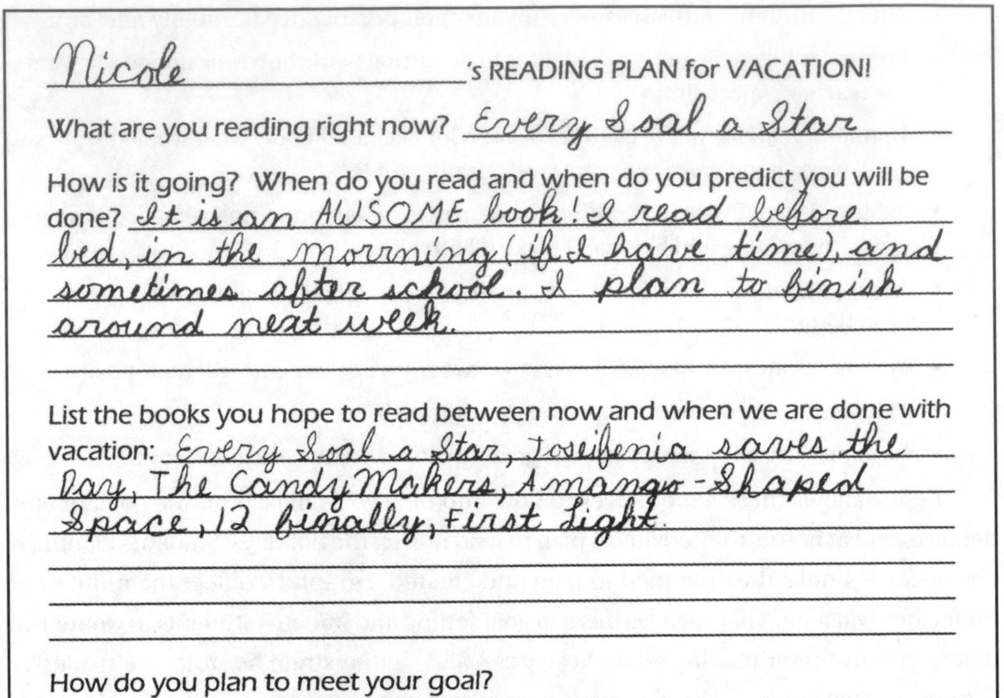

_Nicole_____ 's READING PLAN for VACATION!

What are you reading right now? _Every Soal a Star_

How is it going? When do you read and when do you predict you will be done? _It is an AWSOME book! I read before bed, in the morning (if I have time), and sometimes after school. I plan to finish around next week._

List the books you hope to read between now and when we are done with vacation: _Every Soal a Star, Joseifenia saves the Day, The Candy Makers, A mango-Shaped Space, 12 finally, First Light._

How do you plan to meet your goal?

I will read AT LEAST for 30 minutes in bed. I will read for as much time I have until breakfast so I can wake up a little. I will also read during the day when I don't know "what to do with myself".

What help might you need?

I need to see what kinds of books I need for the genra challenge. I need to go to the library to see what kinds of books I need to finish the challenge.

FIGURE 5.29 **A written plan allows students to work toward manageable goals**

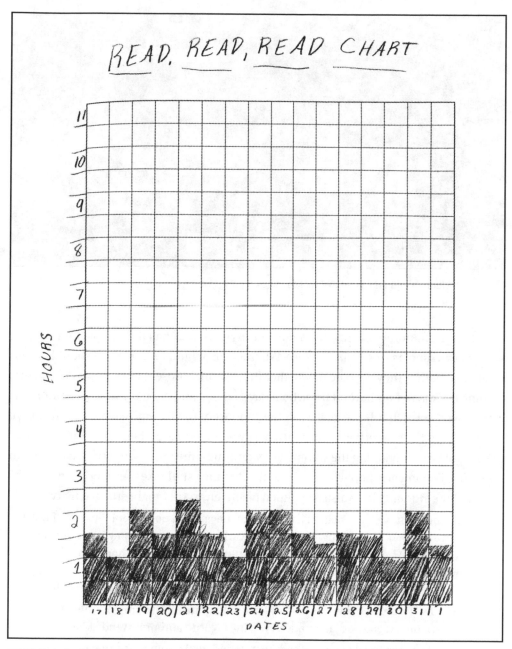

FIGURE 5.30 **Students create a graph to visually set and achieve vacation reading goals**

FIGURE 5.31 **Hannah and Erin share their holiday book plan**

Too often, home reading goals reflect busywork that has little impact on reading such as worksheets or trivial activities. Whether for school *or* home, we should always evaluate whether they are cute or whether they "count" (Roser 2001). Lesley knows that reading counts in and beyond the school day and has made it a priority. This priority is also viewed as a schoolwide goal. With the support of the Parent Teacher Organization, every child in the school will leave with a baggy of ten books of their choice at the end of the school year. Increasing the volume of reading at home and giving students access to books has become a schoolwide goal that the Sunapee staff takes very seriously.

Lesley's students have also responded positively to this goal-setting activity:

- Hannah: "It was very helpful having a plan because I know after I finish my book I have another one waiting. Having my vacation plan lets me know I am ready for vacation. When I showed my dad and a student on the high-school soccer team where he works, he said: 'Hannah is going to be smart and score goals!' Do you know what that feels like? I felt *so* proud!" (That's our ultimate goal, Hannah.)

- Nicole: "I wanted the books I have because they are all (six) from Wendy Mass— except one. If you have not noticed yet, my favorite author is Wendy Mass."

- Jake: "I chose these books because they sounded like something that would get me into it."

- Matthew: "This weekend I got in more reading than usual."

- Will: "I think that the reading plan is very helpful because I always know what book I am going to be reading next now. That makes me excited to read more."

- Sean: "I like it—I don't always get reading in. I like that this plan gives me an idea of when I will read. It helps me get it in."
- Maddy: "I liked that I knew what to read next. Plus if I didn't like the book I had a backup. I really liked this idea."

Lesley's excitement also inspired her to create a blog after they received a letter asking about book recommendations (http://whatismynextbook.blogspot.com). The blog has grown almost overnight, and her students read the letters to recommend books and research new books. They are even inviting panels of students at every grade level to come with their books to educate them about what younger readers want. Are Lesley's efforts to get her kids reading more making a difference? You decide.

Hogwarts or District 12 is where I shall be. I am a reader. I visit my friends a good amount of time and go through castles and forests. When I find new friends I stick with them. When I read I am in places like Minneapolis with my friends Jack and Hazel. By the time I'm dead I will have made 1000s of friends and found 1000s of new places. I am a reader!

—Sean (Note: All references are characters/places from books Sean read this year.)

A reader is someone who can get lost in a book easily and won't let anything distract her. A reader is someone who knows what she wants to read next and won't let anything get in her way to get that book. A reader is someone who can read fluently and with lots of expression. A reader is someone who will really read and not just go home and fake it. A reader is someone who can get lost in a book and read for hours.

—Hannah

A reader is someone who reads every second she can. A reader is someone who has a plan and sticks with it. She gets lost in her just-right books. She doesn't need a picture on the page, she has one in her mind. She wants to be surrounded by books rather than electronics. She uses thinking strategies to help guide her though the book.

—Nicole

Lesley is living and breathing what she wants for her students. As she sets her own goals and then helps her students do the same, she assumes responsibility personally and to her students. She can only find the time to accomplish these critical and lasting goals because she is willing to say "yes" to the things that matter and "no" to the things that don't. Lesley knows what matters and she fills each day pursuing those things.

Using the Potent Transformative Process to Increase Our Instructional Curiosity

George Loewenstein of Carnegie Melon University says that curiosity happens when we are spurred to fill a gap in existing knowledge (1994). This sense of curiosity defines assessment as a potent transformative tool as we actively seek to satisfy our own curiosity about student learning and use these new understandings to increase the quality of our teaching. An increasing knowledge makes us even more curious, which leads us to seek yet more knowledge. Our curiosity thus leads to improved teaching *and* learning.

FIGURE 5.32 **Photographs displayed that reflect each stage on the assessment wall allow literacy consultant Jo Skarin and Title 1 teacher Debbie Shapiro to visually see the progress students have made throughout the year**

Transformative assessment in the dual role described in this chapter is sorely needed. We can only accomplish this if we can impact both student *and* teacher learning as we consider how to move students forward *and* elevate our understandings. Pearson suggests we may need an "endangered species act" for literacy since "in our rush to account- ability, we have created such a tight link between instruction and assessment that we have made a mockery of the whole notion of transfer of learning as the gold standard to which all students and teach- ers should aspire" (Pearson 2007, 145–146).

Each of the dedicated teachers in this and pre- vious chapters embodies assessment as a potent transformative process—the very foundation of great work. They refuse to view assessment in passive terms and insist on using it to inform learning *and* teaching. They are more aware of their students' suc- cesses and needs and of themselves as learners. Their students grow because *they* are willing to grow alongside them. In the end, great work is just that simple and just that complicated. And my oh my, what a privilege it is to behold this wonderfully mag- ical undertaking in action!

CHAPTER 6

Sustaining Our Great Work as We Keep the Momentum Going

> ❝ *Great work is innovative, inventive. It goes beyond today and influences tomorrow. You know the work is great when you can't stop thinking about it. Great work empowers people to take action. Great work is memorable. It causes disequilibrium. Great work inspires others to do the impossible. It removes excuses and focuses on change."*

(LINDA DORN, EMAIL MESSAGE TO AUTHOR, SEPTEMBER 4, 2011)

Linda has brilliantly captured the very essence of this book. Great work impacts our students' future instructional landscape. Great work captures our thoughts and leaves us wanting more. Great work induces discomfort, combined with unstoppable resolve, to reach sheer heights of excellence. Great work is innovative, inventive, empowering, memorable, and inspiring. Great work is—well, *teachers focusing on the literacy work that matters.*

The definition of *change* illustrates the choice before us: to give up something in exchange for something else. Excellent teachers *choose* to alleviate bad work so they can choose to do great work. Excellent teachers *choose* what will enter their day so they can choose what will not. Excellent teachers *choose* to ensure the success of every student every day. Even when turmoil surrounds them, excellent teachers *choose* great work.

Bad work is not about being a "bad" teacher. We all succumb to bad work at one time or another for one reason or another. But if bad work outweighs good work and great work because we fail to recognize it or continue doing it intentionally once we do, this dangerous imbalance affects our impact in negative ways. We have a dual purpose of knowing what *is* working and what *is not* working. Reading specialist Jamie Berry of Rochester, Minnesota, captures this purpose:

> *There are many books that tell us what best practice is; but for the first time someone is telling us what best practice is not. Thanks to Mary's insight into bad work,*

*good work, and great work in the area of literacy, we can be reflective in our prac-
tices and make the necessary changes to do the great work that matters most to our
students. (email message to author, December 7, 2011)*

But how do we distinguish the quality of our work? Rick Wormeli brilliantly highlights this distinction using two opposing perspectives:

*Bad work mires us in what we already are, limiting our perspective as we stare at
two-dimensional silhouettes dancing on a back cavern wall. We find little hope in
disconnected skills and content, yet our daily diet of disconnection is somehow
comforting; it's familiar and we don't have to engage. Instead, we massage our ego
on false presumptions of black-and-white truth, protecting our personal status
quo for one more day.*

   *Great work ignites aspiration. It reveals the tools we heretofore couldn't see or
use, and provides catalysts to use them meaningfully. As students doing great work,
we admit to classmates we'd do this work even if it wasn't required by the teacher.
We respond to parents' evening inquiries about the day's learning in paragraphs,
not grunts. The possibility of doing great work in the future is reason enough to set
the morning alarm. (email message to author, January 2, 2012)*

You see, bad work is an opportunity to alter our course and explore more great work
possibilities ahead, as described in *Beautiful Oops!* (Saltzberg 2010):

When you think you have made a mistake. Oops!

Think of it as an opportunity to make something beautiful.

The dedicated teachers in this book made a choice to critically examine potential
"Oops!" and turn them into something beautiful. They are a testament to the thoughtful
responsive instruction that moves us to do more great work by refusing to make excuses
that obstruct our course. They changed because they made a choice to change. They
made a choice to say "no" to the wrong things so they could say "yes" to the right things.
The very moment we enter our learning day we are in control of the choices that matter.

So let's look at our final reflection form to see how two spotlight teachers made
choices. Our final form, Timeline of Personal Professional Growth Transformation, allows
you to take a look back to celebrate your growth process so that you will never lose sight
of the changes that have become rooted in your work.

Title 1 teacher Debbie Shapiro in Sunapee, New Hampshire, divided her then-and-
now pies at the top of the form based on small-group instruction (see Figure 6.1). Debbie

has eliminated round-robin reading, instead opting for deeper, more thoughtful conversations using instructional or independent texts. She decreased the size of groups, initiated more focused word work, and added a writing component. Debbie admits it took time to recognize the value of increasing the volume of reading, but now it's her priority. Quite an accomplishment, wouldn't you say!

Debbie's colleague, fifth-grade teacher Lesley Scheele, completed her then-and-now pies based on her changing percentage of bad work, good work, and great work (see Figure 6.2). Lesley recognized bad work she needed to erase in order to do more great work. She did this by teaching smarter, not harder. Lesley devotes more time to one-to-one and small groups and she uses whole-class focus lessons to introduce new learning concepts. Lesley has an altered perception of her teaching—"I constantly think now: What am I doing that is working? How can it be better? What can I get rid of?"

Debbie, Lesley, and all of the spotlight teachers in this book have changed since we began our journey together. They have changed because their great work is now the principle upon which everything they do is based. Covey describes this lasting nature of principles: "They can't pave our way with shortcuts and quick fixes. They don't depend on the behavior of others, the environment, or the current fad for their validity. Principles don't die. They aren't here one day and gone the next." (2004, 22) Each of these teachers is forever changed because good to great work is the principle they now live by.

Our spotlight teachers have modeled each of our forms, but my goal is for you to use them to generate your own great-work principles. As you reflect on your learning journey, the forms will give you a concrete record of your move from bad to good to great work. Like Debbie, you may focus on one aspect of your teaching where you can make the greatest impact at that time according to your goals and level of readiness. Or like Lesley, you may want to take a more global look at your teaching. Either way, the forms allow you to put your goals and celebrations in writing so you can continuously reflect on what is working and what is not working, what changes you need to make or have made, and how you can continue to develop new changes along the way.

Great work is a never-ending proposition that requires ongoing effort to sustain so that it can become a principle. This process varies as described by Sharon Taberski:

> Great work gives you something solid to stand on and think from. Like a wonderful theory, it doesn't lay out precisely how to proceed but simply inspires you to do some great thinking and work of your own. (email message to author, December 21, 2011)

Timeline of Personal Professional Growth Transformation

Name _Deb Shapiro_   Dates: _Jan._ to _Present time_

What did your Pie Chart look like then?	What does your Pie Chart look like now?
Small group instruction 30 mins — Sight Word practice, Dis., Round Robin Reading, word work, writing	K — Meaningful discussion, new text, writing, Re-read, Word work, poems, fluency practise, use of LLI program

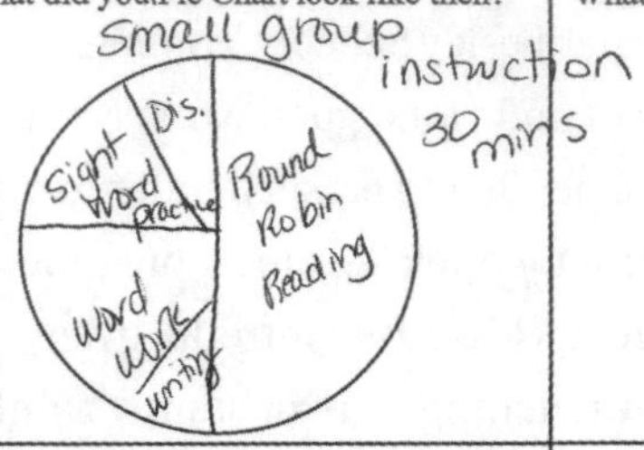

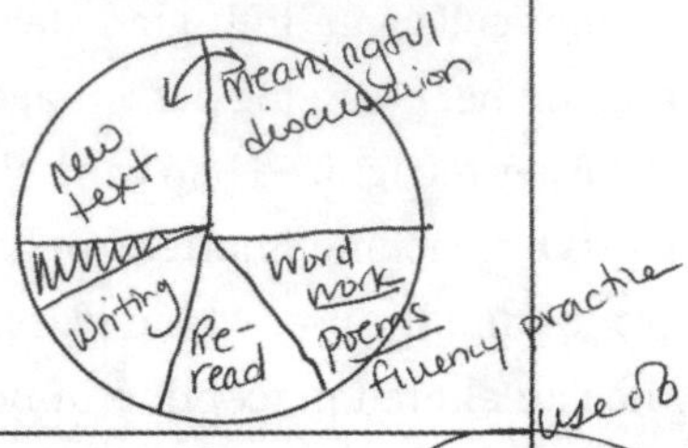

Then	Now
It took an awful long time for me to realize that 80% more reading gets done during RR reading.	The importance of Comprehension conversations Quick, focused instruction on Word work
my groups were also larger, much less discussions were taking place.	Re-reads/new reads NO RR reading. Reading in head, knowing how to whisper read.

How has your role as a reflective teacher transformed your instructional practices?

Working with you has solidified my view of how important, focused planned instruction is for 30 minutes. My groups are no more than _3_ children. I make sure we always have a conversation about the story/include a writing piece. Also, the importance of making children aware of how important time on task during 30 minutes is. Focused, planned, routine, procedure . . .

FIGURE 6.1 **Debbie reflects on how she has increased the quality of her small-group instruction**

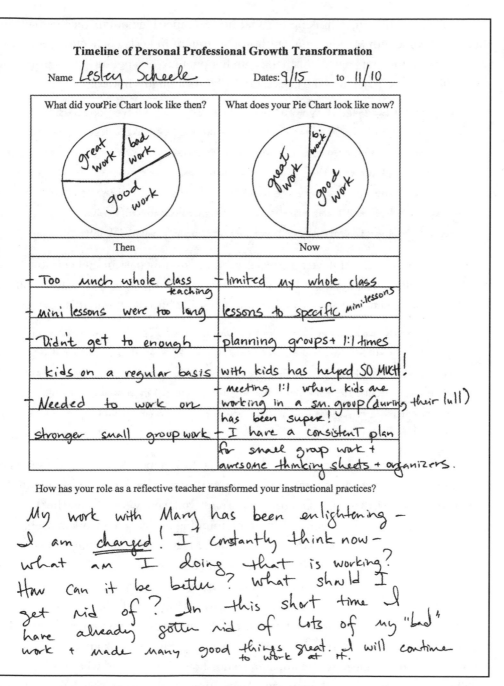

Timeline of Personal Professional Growth Transformation

Name _Lesley Scheele_   Dates: _9/15_ to _11/10_

What did your Pie Chart look like then?	What does your Pie Chart look like now?
great work / bad work / good work	great work / b work / good work
Then	Now
- Too much whole class teaching	- limited my whole class
- Mini lessons were too long	lessons to specific mini-lessons
- Didn't get to enough	- planning groups + 1:1 times
kids on a regular basis	with kids has helped SO MUCH!
- Needed to work on	- meeting 1:1 when kids are working in a sm. group (during their lull) has been super!
stronger small group work	- I have a consistent plan for small group work + awesome thinking sheets + organizers.

How has your role as a reflective teacher transformed your instructional practices?

My work with Mary has been enlightening —
I am _changed_! I constantly think now —
what am I doing that is working?
How can it be better? What should I
get rid of? In this short time I
have already gotten rid of lots of my "bad"
work + made many good things great. I will continue
to work at it.

FIGURE 6.2 **Lesley reflects on how she has achieved more great work**

To illustrate this great thinking, we'll see how Sunapee Elementary teachers sustain their great work with Maddy, a new fifth-grade student in Lesley Scheele's classroom. Maddy graced the first page of this book with her poem. When her insightful principal, Alan Pullman, asked her how she likes school, Maddy thoughts flowed:

> They don't judge me. They treat me like I've been going here for years. I have glasses, but they see me for who I am inside. I felt like a loser at my old school because the smartest kids were the teacher's pet. Mrs. Scheele doesn't have pets and she took time to get to know me and she's super funny. We get advanced material because she wants us to learn more. I didn't learn much at my old school and I was always confused. I could only write what my teacher told me to write there but now I get to write what I want.

Einstein once said, "I have no special talent. I am only passionately curious." We need passionate curiosity to achieve great work. My own passionate curiosity about Maddy led me to a conversation with her about how her life changed in this new school:

> Reading feels like another dimension now. When I read I feel like I'm in the book. I want to scream at the characters, "No, don't do it!" Sometimes I can't put a book down. It's like trick or treating because you don't want to stop. I love books with great detail. The more you read, the more your schema grows. You can add onto it more and more and it gives you great ideas about writing too. I love to write because it's a great way to express your feelings. Poetry is my favorite.

How fortunate this amazing young lady moved to Sunapee, New Hampshire, where her potential was immediately recognized and nurtured. Thank you, Mr. Pullman, for caring enough to ask that important question. Thank you, Lesley, for allowing her to shine in your presence. And thank you, Maddy, for reminding us that great work matters.

When Steve Jobs addressed the 2005 graduating class at Stanford University he said, "The only way to be truly satisfied is to do what you believe is great work." That message has resonated in my mind as I saw this book transform from an impassioned vision to an exhilarating reality. Then two unexpected surprises happened along the way.

As I watched these remarkable teachers change in ways even they did not anticipate, I too changed. I am indebted to the amazing teachers in Mustang, Oklahoma; Rochester, Minnesota; and Sunapee, New Hampshire, who showed this ol' girl what instructional excellence is all about through their eyes. An exciting collaboration with dedicated educators breathed life into each page of this book—and I am forever changed!

As if this life-altering collaboration wasn't enough, one of my most memorable students magically reappeared in my life. After looking for me for over twenty years, Aisha recently surprised me with words that filled my heart with joy:

> *It is rare that a student has even one teacher make a lasting impression. You were that teacher for me. You connected with me not just on an educational level, but at the heart level. I never forgot you or your words of encouragement. (Aisha, email message to author, December 8, 2011)*

Aisha's words spoke to the heart and soul of my work with these wonderful teachers and reminds me of the tremendous impact we have on students. *We choose* to touch their lives in ways we may not even be privy to at the time. *We choose* to connect at an educational level and a heart level. For better or worse, *we choose*. Aisha's words reflect what these teachers embrace at the center of their teaching—*our choices matter*.

So what did I learn about great work? Like Linda, I learned great work is about being innovative, inventive, empowering, memorable, and inspiring. I learned great work is about saying "yes" to the things that matter and "no" to the things that don't. I learned great work is about intentional good to great teaching. I learned great work is about *focusing on the literacy work that matters*.

What did I learn? Well . . . what I learned could fill a book. And that, my friend, is my gift to you because only you can achieve the great work our students deserve—*every* day with *every* child!

Adler, D. A. 2010. *A Little at a Time.* New York: Holiday House.

Allington, R. L. 2002. "What I've Learned About Effective Reading Instruction from a Decade of Studying Exemplary Elementary Classroom Teachers." *Phi Delta Kappan* 83 (10): 740–47.

———. 2009. *What Really Matters in Response to Intervention.* Boston, MA: Pearson.

———, ed. 2010. *Essential Readings on Struggling Learners.* Newark, DE: International Reading Association.

———. 2011. "What At-Risk Readers Need." *Educational Leadership* 68 (6): 40–45.

———. 2012a. *What Really Matters for Struggling Readers: Designing Research-Based Programs.* 3rd ed. Boston, MA: Pearson.

———. 2012b. "Struggling Does Not Mean Learning Disabled." *Reading Today* 29 (5): 35.

Allington, R. L., and R. E. Gabriel. 2012. "Every Child, Every Day." *Educational Leadership* 69 (6): 10–15.

Allington, R. L., and P. H. Johnston. 2002. *Reading to Learn: Lessons from Exemplary Fourth-Grade Classrooms.* New York: Guilford.

Allington, R. L., P. H. Johnston, and J. P. Day. 2002. "Exemplary Fourth-Grade Teachers." *Language Arts* 79: 462–66.

Allington, R. L., and A. McGill-Franzen. 2010. "Why So Much Oral Reading?" In *Revisiting Silent Reading: New Directions for Teachers and Researchers*, eds. E. H. Hiebert and D. R. Reutzel, 45–56. Newark, DE: International Reading Association.

Allington, R. L., and P. D. Pearson. 2011. "The Casualties of Policy on Early Literacy Development." *Language Arts* 89 (1): 70–74.

Applegate, A. J., M. D. Applegate, and J. D. Turner. 2010. "Learning Disabilities or Teaching Disabilities? Rethinking Literacy Failure." *The Reading Teacher* 64 (3): 211–13.

Applegate, A. J., M. D. Applegate, and V. B. Modla. 2009. "'She's My Best Reader; She Just Can't Comprehend': Studying the Relationship Between Fluency and Comprehension." *The Reading Teacher* 62 (6): 512–21.

Ash, G. E., M. R. Kuhn, and S. Walpole. 2009. "Analyzing 'Inconsistencies' in Practice: Teachers' Continued Use of Round Robin Reading." *Reading & Writing Quarterly* 25 (1): 87–103.

Atwell, N. 2007. *The Reading Zone: How to Help Kids Become Skilled, Passionate, Habitual, Critical Readers.* New York: Scholastic.

———. 2011. *Reading in the Middle Workshop.* DVD-ROM. Portsmouth, NH: Heinemann.

Betts, E. A. 1946. *Foundations of Reading Instruction: With Emphasis on Differentiated Guidance.* New York: American Book.

Black, P., and D. Wiliam. 1998. "Inside the Black Box: Raising Standards Through Classroom Assessment." *Phi Delta Kappan* 80 (2): 139–44, 146–48.

———. 2010. "A Pleasant Surprise." *Phi Delta Kappan* 92 (1): 47–48.

Blauman, L. 2011. *The Inside Guide to the Reading-Writing Classroom: Strategies for Extraordinary Teaching.* Portsmouth, NH: Heinemann.

Boudett, K. P., E. A. City, and R. J. Murnane, eds. 2010. *Data Wise: A Step-by-Step Guide to Using Assessment Results to Improve Teaching and Learning.* Cambridge, MA: Harvard Education Press.

Boushey, G., and J. Moser. 2006. *Daily Five: Fostering Literacy Independence in the Elementary Grades.* Portland, ME: Stenhouse.

———. 2009. *CAFÉ: Engaging All Students in Daily Literacy Assessment and Instruction.* Portland, ME: Stenhouse.

Bregman, P. 2011. *Eighteen Minutes: Find Your Focus, Master Distraction, and Get the Right Things Done.* New York: Hachette Book Group.

Brown, M. 1998. *Arthur Writes a Story: An Arthur Adventure.* Arthur Adventure Series. Boston, MA: Little Brown Books for Young Readers.

Buffum, A., M. Mattos, and C. Weber. 2010. "The Why Behind RTI." *Educational Leadership* 68 (2): 10–16.

Bunting, E. 1992. *The Wall.* San Anselmo, CA: Sandpiper.

Burkins, J. M., and M. M. Croft. 2010. *Preventing Misguided Reading: New Strategies for Guided Reading Teachers.* Thousand Oaks, CA: International Reading Association.

Calkins, L. M. 2001. *The Art of Teaching Reading.* New York: Longman.

Campbell Hill, B., and C. Ekey. 2010. *The Next-Step Guide to Enriching Classroom Environments: Rubrics and Resources for Self-Evaluation and Goal Setting for Literacy Coaches, Principals, and Teacher Study Groups, K–6.* Portsmouth, NH: Heinemann.

Clay, M. 1985. *The Early Detection of Reading Difficulties.* Portsmouth, NH: Heinemann.

———. 1987. "Learning to Be Learning Disabled." *New Zealand Journal of Educational Studies* 22 (2): 155–73.

Collins, J. 2001. *Good to Great: Why Some Companies Make the Leap . . . and Others Don't.* New York: Harper Business.

Cooter, R. B., and H. Perkins. 2011. "Much Done, Much Yet to Do." *The Reading Teacher* 64 (8): 563–66.

Covey, S. R. 2004. *The 7 Habits of Highly Effective People: Powerful Lessons in Personal Change.* New York: Free Press.

Dewitz, P., S. B. Leahy, J. Jones, and P. M. Sullivan. 2010. *The Essential Guide to Selecting and Using Core Reading Programs.* Newark, DE: International Reading Association.

Dirksen, D. J. 2011. "Hitting the Reset Button: Using Formative Assessment to Guide Instruction." *Phi Delta Kappan* 92 (7): 26–31.

Dorn, L. J., and B. Schubert. 2008. "A Comprehensive Intervention Model for Preventing Reading Failure: A Response to Intervention Process." *Journal of Reading Recovery* 7 (2): 29–41.

Dorn, L. J., and C. Soffos. 2012. *Interventions That Work: A Comprehensive Intervention Model for Preventing Reading Failure in Grades K–3.* Boston, MA: Pearson.

Duke, N., and N. M. Martin. 2011. "10 Things Every Literacy Educator Should Know About Research." *The Reading Teacher* 65 (1): 9–22.

Edwards, P. 2011. "Access to Books Makes a Difference." *Reading Today* 28 (6): 16.

Enriquez, G., S. Jones, and L. W. Clarke. 2010. "Turning Around Our Perceptions and Practices, Then Our Readers." *The Reading Teacher* 64 (1): 73–76.

Fisher, D., and N. Frey. 2008. *Better Learning Through Structured Teaching: A Framework for the Gradual Release of Responsibility.* Alexandria, VA: Association for Supervision and Curriculum Development.

Fountas, I. C., and G. S. Pinnell. 2008a. Leveled Literacy Intervention Orange System. Portsmouth, NH: Heinemann.

———. 2008b. Leveled Literacy Intervention Green System. Portsmouth, NH: Heinemann.

———. 2008c. Leveled Literacy Intervention Blue System. Portsmouth, NH: Heinemann.

———. 2010a. Benchmark Assessment System 1. 2nd ed. Portsmouth, NH: Heinemann.

———. 2010b. Benchmark Assessment System 2. 2nd ed. Portsmouth, NH: Heinemann.

Fullan, M. 2002. "The Change Leader." *Educational Leadership* 59 (8): 16–21.

———. 2008. *The Six Secrets of Change: What the Best Leaders Do to Help Their Organizations Survive and Thrive.* San Francisco, CA: Jossey-Bass.

Fullan, M., A. Bertani, and J. Quinn. 2004. "New Lessons for Districtwide Reform." *Educational Leadership* 61 (7): 43–46.

Gabriel, R., J. P. Day, and R. Allington. 2011. "Exemplary Teacher Voices on Their Own Development." *Phi Delta Kappan* 92 (8): 37–41.

Gallagher, K. 2009. *Readicide: How Schools Are Killing Reading and What You Can Do About It.* Portland, ME: Stenhouse.

Gambrell, L. B., J. A. Malloy, and S. A. Mazzoni. 2011. "Evidence-Based Best Practices in Comprehensive Literacy Instruction." In *Best Practices in Literacy Instruction.* 4th ed., eds. L. M. Morrow and L. B. Gambrell, 11–36. New York: Guilford Press.

Gindis, B. 1999. "Vygotsky's Vision: Reshaping the Practice of Special Education for the 21st Century." *Remedial and Special Education* 20 (6): 32–64.

Gladwell, M. 2002. *The Tipping Point: How Little Things Can Make a Big Difference.* New York: Little Brown and Company.

Glaser, M. 2008. *Art Is Work.* New York: Overlook Press.

Godin, S. 2007. *The Dip: A Little Book That Teaches You When to Quit (and When to Stick).* New York: Portfolio.

Goodman, K. 1969. "Analysis of Oral Reading Miscues: Applied Psycholinguistics." In *Language and Literacy: The Selected Writings of Kenneth Goodman.* Vol. 1. ed. F. Gollasch, 123–24. Boston: Routledge & Kegan Paul.

———. 1973. "Miscues: Windows on the Reading Process." In *Miscue Analysis: Applications to Reading Instruction,* ed. K. Goodman, 3–14. Urbana, IL: National Council of Teachers of English.

Goodman, Y. 1978. "Kidwatching: Observing Children in the Classroom." In *Observing the Language Learner,* eds. A. Jagger and M. T. Smith-Burke, 9–18. Newark, DE: International Reading Association.

Guskey, T. R. 2011. "Five Obstacles to Grading Reform." *Educational Leadership* 69 (3): 16–21.

Hammond, W. D., and D. D. Nessell. 2011. *The Comprehension Experience: Engaging Readers Through Effective Inquiry and Discussion.* Portsmouth, NH: Heinemann.

Harris, T. L., and R. E. Hodges, eds. 1995. *The Literacy Dictionary: The Vocabulary of Reading and Writing.* Newark, DE: International Reading Association.

Harvey, S., and A. Goudvis. 2007. *Strategies That Work: Teaching Comprehension for Understanding and Engagement.* Portland, ME: Stenhouse.

———. 2008. *The Primary Comprehension Toolkit: Language and Literacy Lessons for Active Literacy (Teacher's Guide).* Portsmouth, NH: firsthand/Heinemann.

Heritage, M. 2007. "Formative Assessment: What Do Teachers Need to Know and Do?" *Phi Delta Kappan* 89 (2): 140–45.

Hiebert, E. H., and D. R. Reutzel, eds. 2010. *Revisiting Silent Reading: New Directions for Teachers and Researchers.* Newark, DE: International Reading Association.

Hollimon, D. 2011. "It's Simple: Read More, Write More, Teach Vocabulary." *Reading Today* 28 (4): 13.

Howard, M. 2009. *RTI from All Sides: What Every Teacher Needs to Know.* Portsmouth, NH: Heinemann.

———. 2010. *Moving Forward with RTI: Reading and Writing Activities for Every Instructional Setting and Tier.* Portsmouth, NH: Heinemann.

Hoyt, L., K. Davis, J. Olson, and K. Boswell. 2011. *Solutions for Reading Comprehension: Strategic Interventions for Striving Learners.* Portsmouth, NH: Heinemann.

International Reading Association. 2010. *Standards for Reading Professionals: A Reference for the Preparation of Educators in the United States.* Rev. ed. Newark, DE: International Reading Association.

International Reading Association and National Council of Teachers of English. 2010. *Standards for the Assessment of Reading and Writing.* Rev. ed. Newark, DE: International Reading Association.

Johnson, P. 2006. *One Child at a Time: Making the Most of Your Time with Struggling Readers, K–6.* Portland, ME: Stenhouse.

Johnson, P., and K. Keier. 2010. *Catching Readers Before They Fall: Supporting Readers Who Struggle, K–4.* Portland, ME: Stenhouse.

Johnston, P. H. 2004. *Choice Words: How Our Language Affects Children's Learning.* Portland, ME: Stenhouse.

———. 2012. *Opening Minds: Using Language to Change Lives.* Portland, ME: Stenhouse.

Keene, E., and S. Zimmerman. 2007. *Mosaic of Thought: The Power of Comprehension Strategy Instruction.* 2nd ed. Portsmouth, NH: Heinemann.

Kotter, J. P. 2008. *A Sense of Urgency.* Boston, MA: Harvard Business Press.

Krashen, S. 2004. *The Power of Reading: Insights from the Research.* 2nd ed. Portsmouth, NH: Heinemann.

———. 2011. *Free Voluntary Reading.* Santa Barbara, CA: Libraries Unlimited.

Loewenstein, G. 1994. "The Psychology of Curiosity: A Review and Reinterpretation." *Psychological Bulletin* 116 (1): 75–98.

Luntz, F. I. 2011. *WIN: The Key Principles to Take Your Business from Ordinary to Extraordinary.* New York: Hyperion.

Marzano, R. J. 2011/2012. "It's How You Use a Strategy." *Educational Leadership* 69 (4): 88–89.

Marzano, R. J., D. J. Pickering, and J. E. Pollock. 2004. *Classroom Instruction That Works: Research-Based Strategies for Increasing Student Achievement.* Upper Saddle River, NJ: Prentice Hall.

McQuillan, J. 2008. *The Literacy Crisis: False Claims, Real Solutions.* Portsmouth, NH: Heinemann.

Miller, D. 2002. *Reading with Meaning: Teaching Comprehension in the Primary Grades.* Portland, ME: Stenhouse.

———. 2008. *Teaching with Intention: Defining Beliefs, Aligning Practice, and Taking Action, K–5.* Portland, ME: Stenhouse.

Miller, D. 2009. *The Book Whisperer: Awakening the Inner Reader in Every Child.* San Francisco, CA: Jossey-Bass.

Morrow, L. M. 2010. "Ask the Expert." *The Reading Teacher* 64 (2): 140.

National Institute of Child Health and Human Development. 2000. *Teaching Children to Read: An Evidence-Based Assessment of the Scientific Research Literature of Reading and Its Implications for Reading Instruction.* NIH Publication No. 00-4769. Washington, DC: U.S. Government Printing Office.

Neuman., S., and D. K. Dickinson, eds. 2011. *Handbook of Early Literacy Research.* Vol. 3. New York: Guilford Press.

Newkirk, T. 2009. *Holding on to Good Ideas in a Time of Bad Ones: Six Literacy Principles Worth Fighting For.* Portsmouth, NH: Heinemann.

———. 2012. *The Art of SLOW Reading.* Portsmouth, NH: Heinemann.

Opitz, M. F., M. P. Ford, and J. A. Erekson. 2011. *Accessible Assessment: How Nine Sensible Techniques Can Power Data-Driven Reading Instruction.* Portsmouth, NH: Heinemann.

Pearson, P. D. 2007. "An Endangered Species Act for Literacy Education." *Journal of Literacy Research* 39 (2): 145–62.

Pearson, P. D., and M. Gallagher. 1983. "The Instruction of Reading Comprehension." *Contemporary Educational Psychology* 8 (3): 317–344.

Petty, G. 2009. *Evidence-Based Teaching: A Practical Approach.* 2nd ed. Cheltenham, UK: Nelson Thornes.

Pinnell, G. S., and I. C. Fountas. 2009. *When Readers Struggle: Teaching That Works.* Portsmouth, NH: Heinemann.

Pressley, M. 2007. "Achieving Best Practices." In *Best Practices in Literacy Instruction*, eds. L. B. Gambrell, L. M. Morrow, and M. Pressley, 397–404. New York: Guilford Press.

Rasinski, T., and P. Hamman. 2010. "Fluency: Why It Is 'Not Hot.'" *Reading Today* 28 (1): 26.

Reutzel, D. R., and R. Cooter. 2011. *Teaching Children to Read: The Teacher Makes the Difference.* 6th ed. New York: Allyn & Bacon.

Roam, D. 2011. *Blah Blah Blah: What to Do When Words Don't Work.* New York: Portfolio/Penguin.

Roser, N. L. 2001. "A Place for Everything and Literature in Its Place." *The New Advocate* 14 (3): 211–21.

Saltzberg, B. 2010. *Beautiful Oops!* New York: Workman Publishing.

Scanlon, D. M., and K. L. Anderson. 2010. "Using the Interactive Strategies Approach to Prevent Reading Difficulties in an RTI Context." In *Successful Approaches to RTI: Collaborative Practices for Improving K–12 Literacy*, eds. M. Y. Lipson and K. K. Wixson, 20–65. Newark, DE: International Reading Association.

Schmoker, M. 2001. "The 'Crayola Curriculum.'" *Education Week*, October 24.

———. 2004. "Tipping Point: From Feckless Reform to Substantive Instructional Improvement." *Phi Delta Kappan* 85 (6): 424–32.

———. 2009. "What Money Can't Buy: Powerful, Overlooked Opportunities for Learning." *Phi Delta Kappan* 90 (7): 524–27.

———. 2011a. *Focus: Elevating the Essentials to Radically Improve Student Learning.* Alexandria, VA: Association for Supervision and Curriculum Development.

———. 2011b. "Hiding in Plain Sight." *Phi Delta Kappan* 93 (1): 68–69.

Serafini, F. 2011. "Creating Space for Children's Literature." *The Reading Teacher* 65 (1): 30–34.

Serravallo, J. 2010. *Teaching Reading in Small Groups: Differentiated Instruction for Building Strategic Independent Readers.* Portsmouth, NH: Heinemann.

Spence, R. M. Jr. 2009. *It's Not What You Sell, It's What You Stand For: Why Every Extraordinary Business Is Driven by Purpose.* New York: Portfolio.

Stanier, M. B. 2008. *Find Your Great Work: Napkin-Size Solutions to Stop the Busywork. Start the Work That Matters.* Toronto, ON: Box of Crayons Press.

———. 2010. *Do More Great Work: Stop the Busywork and Start the Work that Matters.* New York: Workman Publishing.

Steele, C. F. 2010/2011. "Inspired Responses." *Educational Leadership* 68 (4): 64–68.

Stevens, J. 1995. *Tops and Bottoms.* New York: Harcourt.

Taberski, S. 2011. *Comprehension from the Ground Up: Simplified, Sensible Instruction for the K–3 Reading Workshop.* Portsmouth, NH: Heinemann.

Taylor, B. M. 2011. *Catching Schools: An Action Guide to Schoolwide Reading Improvement.* Portsmouth, NH: Heinemann.

Taylor, B. M., D. S. Peterson, P. D. Pearson, and M. C. Rodriguez. 2002. "Looking Inside Classrooms: Reflecting on the 'How' as Well as the 'What' in Effective Reading Instruction." *The Reading Teacher* 56 (3): 270–79.

Thomas, R. L. 2011. "My Nine 'Truths' of Data Analysis." *Education Week* (36): 1, 29.

Tomlinson, C. A. 2008. "The Goals of Differentiation." *Educational Leadership* 66 (3): 26–30.

———. 2010/2011. "Notes from an Accidental Teacher." *Educational Leadership* 68 (4): 22–26.

Tomlinson, C. A., and J. McTighe. 2006. *Integrating Differentiated Instruction + Understanding by Design: Connecting Content and Kids.* Alexandria, VA: Association for Supervision and Curriculum Development.

Tompkins, G. 2009. *Literacy for the 21st Century: A Balanced Approach.* 5th ed. Upper Saddle River, NJ: Prentice Hall.

Turner, J. D., A. J. Applegate, and M. D. Applegate. 2009. "Teachers as Literacy Leaders." *The Reading Teacher* 63 (3): 254–56.

———. 2011. "New Teachers as Literacy Leaders." *The Reading Teacher* 64 (7): 550–52.

Vygotsky, L. S. 1978. *Mind in Society: The Development of Higher Psychological Processes.* Cambridge, MA: Harvard University Press.

Wormeli, R. 2006. *Fair Isn't Always Equal: Assessing and Grading in the Differentiated Classroom.* Portland, ME: Stenhouse.

Zemelman, S., H. Daniels, and A. Hyde. 2012. *Best Practice: Bringing Standards to Life in America's Classrooms.* 4th ed. Portsmouth, NH: Heinemann.

Zimmerman, S., and C. Hutchins. 2003. *Seven Keys to Comprehension: How to Help Your Kids Read It and Get It!* New York: Three Rivers Press.